FOR GEORGIA AND CALVIN—
MY TWO MOST AMAZING GIFTS.

Nimbus Publishing Limited
3660 Strawberry Hill Street, Halifax, NS, B3K 5A9
(902) 455-4286 nimbus.ca

Printed and bound in Canada
NB1383
Interior design: Peggy Issenman, Peggy & Co. Design and Jenn Embree
Cover design: Jenn Embree and Heather Bryan
Editor: Emily MacKinnon

Library and Archives Canada Cataloguing in Publication

Title: Amazing Black Atlantic Canadians : inspiring stories of courage and achievement / words by Lindsay Ruck ; art by James Bentley.
Names: Ruck, Lindsay, author. | Bentley, James, 1968- illustrator.
Description: Includes index.
Identifiers: Canadiana (print) 20200268961 | Canadiana (ebook) 2020026897X | ISBN 9781771089173 (softcover) | ISBN 9781771089180 (EPUB)
Subjects: CSH: Black Canadians—Atlantic Provinces—Biography—Juvenile literature. | LCSH: Atlantic Provinces—Biography—Juvenile literature.
Classification: LCC FC2020.B6 Z48 2021 | DDC j971.5/00496—dc23

Nimbus Publishing acknowledges the financial support for its publishing activities from the Government of Canada, the Canada Council for the Arts, and from the Province of Nova Scotia. We are pleased to work in partnership with the Province of Nova Scotia to develop and promote our creative industries for the benefit of all Nova Scotians.

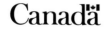 

TABLE OF CONTENTS

INTRODUCTION

What does it mean to be amazing? Someone may be amazing because they're in a hall of fame for reaching greatness in a sport. Others may be amazing because they've written stories or poems that people all around the world will read. Some are called amazing because they've performed in front of thousands of people—some have even shared their talent with kings and queens. Still others are amazing because they've taken a brave stand against **racism** and have used their voice for good. They've helped others in their community any way they can.

As an author, I love discovering fascinating stories about the people and places around me. When I was a girl, my grandfather would tell me stories about how Black soldiers in The Black Battalion struggled to be allowed to fight during the First World War; how the people of Africville were taken away from their beloved community and homes; and how the Black Loyalists first arrived in Atlantic Canada in search of a better life. As a family, we would visit the Black Cultural Centre of Nova Scotia and learn more about **opera singer** Portia White, journalist Carrie Best, and Canadian war hero Jeremiah Jones. My grandfather taught me the importance of Black Canadian history and those conversations are where my journey began in discovering more about the amazing individuals you'll read about in this book.

Working on this book was a big task. I spent a lot of time reading history books and biographies. I did a lot of research on my computer to check facts and gather interesting tidbits. And I spoke with people across the Atlantic provinces who were eager to help me tell these stories. While this book features a lot of Black Atlantic Canadians, it's important to know that not everyone was able to be included in these pages, but that does not mean they are any less amazing. I learned so much about the history of Black people in Atlantic Canada and my hope is that you too will not only learn, but also be inspired by these amazing men, women, and children.

For many of these individuals, it all started with a dream or drive to make a difference. They have worked hard to achieve what some would describe as the impossible. They've jumped over hurdles, broken down barriers, and beaten the odds to achieve greatness. And that is what makes each and every one of them truly amazing.

*Look up definitions to words in **bold** in the glossary,*
beginning on page 148.

PART I

A HISTORY OF BLACK PEOPLE IN ATLANTIC CANADA

> *The legacy...is the legacy of our people–that they had a life here, that they built community here, that this was their home. We have generations of people who are the descendants of Black Loyalists who have been and will continue to be raised in Nova Scotia.*
>
> –Elizabeth Cromwell, historian

> *The more we know about each other, the less we're going to fear each other, the less we're going to have issues with each other, because we're going to recognize that we've all played a part in shaping what is Canada today.*
>
> –Sergeant Craig Smith, RCMP

A HISTORY OF BLACK PEOPLE IN ATLANTIC CANADA

The first recorded Black people in Atlantic Canada date back to the 1600s. Some were brought to the Maritimes as enslaved people, while others arrived as free men and women who were searching for a better life. Moving to a new place and starting all over again isn't always easy—especially if that new place is cold and you are used to warm weather. These men and women had to work very hard to provide for their families. Jobs weren't easy to find, fertile land was hard to come by, and many had to get creative in order to find ways to survive. Some achieved great success in the Atlantic provinces, while others moved on not long after their arrival, but their legacy as the first Blacks in Atlantic Canada lives on through their ancestors. Their tales have been passed down from one generation to the next, so that we do not forget those who came before us and called Nova Scotia, New Brunswick, Newfoundland, or Prince Edward Island home. Their stories, struggles, and triumphs are an important part of Canadian history.

pproximately 350 people from West Africa were captured by French sailors and brought to Île-Royale, Nova Scotia, as enslaved people in the 1600–1700s. The majority of the newcomers lived in Louisbourg, a town that housed a large French military fortress. By 1718, Île-Royale was thriving as a producer and exporter of many goods, including codfish, sugar, molasses, and rum. In 1758, the French settlers renamed the island Cape Breton.

CHARLES

Charles was an eighteen-year-old enslaved boy who lived in Block 2 at Louisbourg in 1773. He was owned by Pierre Benoist, a junior officer at the Fortress of Louisbourg, and his wife, Anne Levron. Charles worked at Pierre and Anne's home, which included a large garden and many farm animals. Charles worked from sun up to sun down and his days were very busy. In the garden, he did all of the planting and weeding, and harvesting of vegetables like potatoes and carrots. He fed all the animals in the sheds, and was also tasked with chopping wood for the stoves and fireplaces inside the home.

Like Charles, most Black men and women during that time worked for white families. Among other jobs, they worked as gardeners, bakers, musicians, soldiers, sailors, fishers, and nursemaids. Enslaved people living on the island all knew one another and spent time together when they weren't working. They would gather for special occasions, like weddings and baptisms. The work was hard and the days were long, but they drew comfort and strength from one another, and through their faith in God.

MARIE MARGUERITE ROSE

arie Marguerite Rose was born in Guinea, a country on the west coast of Africa, and was brought to Louisbourg, Nova Scotia, as an enslaved person in the 1700s. People who were enslaved were often baptized and given a new French name, so at the age of nineteen, she became Marie Maguerite Rose. Marie worked for naval officer Jean Chrysostome Loppinot, taking care of his twelve children and tending to his home.

Marie was freed from slavery in 1755 when she was thirty-eight years old. When someone was freed, it was called **emancipation**. After nineteen years of servitude, Marie was free to live her life as she pleased. She married Jean Baptiste Laurent, a local Mi'kmaw hunter. She was eager to start making money and she found the perfect building in Louisbourg to start her new business—a tavern.

Located at the corner of Saint Louis Street and Place d'Armes, the building was near the barracks of the Fortress of Louisbourg. Marie's former owners and other slaveholders in the community would visit her tavern often. As the owner of the tavern, Marie did it all. She wiped the counters, poured drinks, and counted her earnings at the end of the day.

Marie was also a skilled gardener, cook, and seamstress, and made her own soap and preserves. Sadly, just two years after opening the tavern's doors, Marie passed away in 1757. But her legacy lives on. As a Black woman, Marie beat the odds and became a successful business owner and an important part of her Louisbourg community. Visitors can find a special display celebrating the life of Marie Marguerite Rose at the Fortress of Louisbourg—a reminder of one woman's incredible strength.

MATHIEU DA COSTA

The first recorded free Black person to visit Canada was Mathieu da Costa. He was from the Benin Empire in Nigeria. Mathieu worked as an interpreter for French and Dutch traders and explorers in the early 1600s. Discovering a new piece of land meant meeting new people who didn't always speak the same language. It was common for European explorers to hire African men to act as translators as they explored the African coast. Mathieu spoke French, Dutch, and Portuguese and also worked as an interpreter for Indigenous Peoples in North America. In 1608, Mathieu agreed to work with Pierre Dugua de Monts as an interpreter during his voyages to Canada and Acadia. While we don't know the exact amount, Mathieu was paid quite well for his services. He accompanied Pierre and Samuel de Champlain on at least one of their voyages to Acadia and the St. Lawrence area.

Mathieu's time in Canada has been commemorated at the Port-Royal National Historic Site in Annapolis Royal, Nova Scotia. There is also a school named after Mathieu in Toronto, Ontario, and a street with his name in Montreal and Quebec City. Canada Post made a stamp with Mathieu's picture on it to honour his legacy as the first Black person to arrive in Canada.

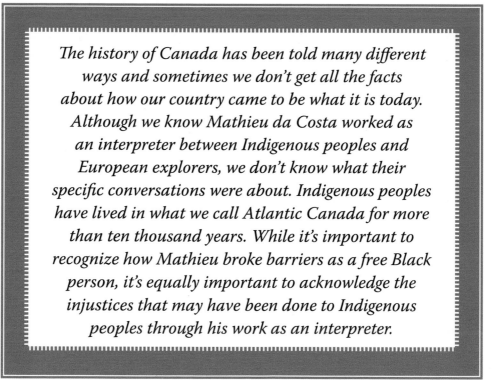

The history of Canada has been told many different ways and sometimes we don't get all the facts about how our country came to be what it is today. Although we know Mathieu da Costa worked as an interpreter between Indigenous peoples and European explorers, we don't know what their specific conversations were about. Indigenous peoples have lived in what we call Atlantic Canada for more than ten thousand years. While it's important to recognize how Mathieu broke barriers as a free Black person, it's equally important to acknowledge the injustices that may have been done to Indigenous peoples through his work as an interpreter.

BLACK LOYALISTS

uring the **American Revolutionary War** of 1775, enslaved Black people were promised "freedom and a farm," which meant a new life and new land if they escaped slavery to join the British Army. These soldiers who escaped were known as Black Loyalists. They were assigned many different duties during the war. Some worked as blacksmiths, shoemakers, and carpenters, while others dug trenches to allow soldiers to move closer to enemy lines. And other men were sent right into the battlefield to fight. Women also played a part in the war efforts. Many worked as nurses and took care of wounded soldiers, while others cooked food and mended clothing.

In 1783, approximately 3,500 Black Loyalists boarded ships leaving New York bound for England, Florida, and Atlantic Canada. The British had promised one hundred acres for each head of household plus an additional fifty acres for each family member. Many landed in Shelburne, Nova Scotia, and the newly free Black Loyalists created their own community in nearby Birchtown. Others settled in Halifax, Annapolis Royal, and Preston. The names of these brave men and women were recorded in a large book called a ledger with the title *Book of Negroes*.

The *Book of Negroes* is roughly 150 pages long, and each handwritten page recorded information on 3,000 Black men, women, and children who travelled on 219 ships sailing from New York between April and November 1783. The *Book of Negroes* recorded the names of enslaved and free Black people who joined the British Army during the American Revolutionary War. Details like a person's approximate age and any illnesses they may have had were also recorded. If your name was in that document, it meant you had been promised a better life as a reward for your loyalty.

But many Black Loyalists were rewarded with broken promises. They never received the land and provisions originally pledged to them, so they were forced to work for very little, taking care of farms or cleaning white people's homes. In 1971, a British company offered to relocate Black Loyalists to Sierra Leone, a country in West Africa. More than one thousand Black Loyalists left Halifax Harbour on-board fifteen ships to find a better life somewhere else.

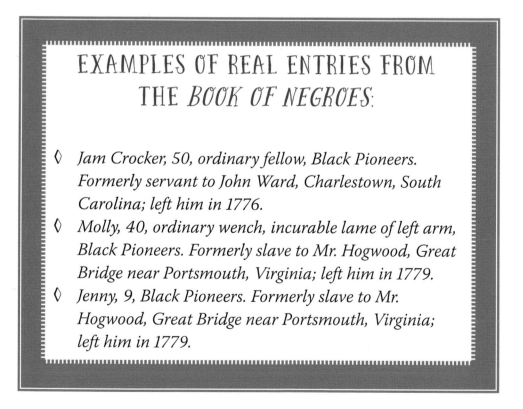

EXAMPLES OF REAL ENTRIES FROM THE *BOOK OF NEGROES*:

◊ *Jam Crocker, 50, ordinary fellow, Black Pioneers. Formerly servant to John Ward, Charlestown, South Carolina; left him in 1776.*
◊ *Molly, 40, ordinary wench, incurable lame of left arm, Black Pioneers. Formerly slave to Mr. Hogwood, Great Bridge near Portsmouth, Virginia; left him in 1779.*
◊ *Jenny, 9, Black Pioneers. Formerly slave to Mr. Hogwood, Great Bridge near Portsmouth, Virginia; left him in 1779.*

WHAT IS A CERTIFICATE OF FREEDOM?

Certificates of Freedom were given to Black Loyalists by British authorities to prove Loyalists had joined the British forces for at least one year during the war. The certificate was meant to ensure they could travel freely to wherever they chose to start a new life free from slavery.

"To the end that peace and good order may the sooner be restored...I do require every person capable of bearing arms to resort to His Majesty's standard... and I do hereby further declare all indented servants, Negroes, or others (appertaining to Rebels) free, that are able and willing to bear arms, they joining His Majesty's Troops, as soon as may be, for the more speedily reducing this Colony to a proper sense of their duty to his Majesty's crown and dignity."

—John Murray was the earl of Dunmore and Virginia's royal governor. His proclamation offered freedom to enslaved people who joined the British army. It was printed in the *Pennsylvania Journal* and *Weekly Advertiser* on December 6, 1775.

GRAND BAY-WESTFIELD

Early settlers of Grand Bay-Westfield, New Brunswick, enslaved Black people who were referred to as "servants." Many of these Black men and women signed long-term contracts, known as indentures, to work in return for passage to the "New World," as some in Europe called North and South America. At the end of the contract, the servant would be free and receive a bit of money and clothing. Settlers from New England brought almost twelve thousand enslaved people with them. Many people who were enslaved became **indentured servants** because the land and supplies that were originally promised to them after joining the British in their war efforts were not granted, and they had very little to survive on. In 1785, thirty-one free people who had been enslaved received a grant of fifty acres in Westfield near Negro Lake and Robin Hood Lake. But the area turned out to be too small and too wooded to grow sufficient crops. Life in Saint John was no better. In 1785, Black people weren't allowed to vote, practise a trade, fish in the harbour, or sell goods. They were also not permitted to live within the city limits unless they worked as menial labourers or servants. By 1790, many abandoned their land and left Westfield. On January 15, 1972, approximately 1,200 free Black people left Halifax in a flotilla and headed for Sierra Leone.

> *Richard Corankapone Wheeler and several of his friends spent fifteen days walking to Halifax from Westfield to catch a ship going to Sierra Leone in western Africa. Many aboard died en route and many of those who survived never received their promised land grants. Those who remained in New Brunswick had to endure discrimination and poverty.*

BLACK ISLANDERS AND THE BOG

The first group of Black men, women, and children arrived on Prince Edward Island as people enslaved by Loyalists who were fleeing the American Revolutionary War in the 1870s. By the early 1900s, most enslaved people had left the Island. But between 1810 and 1900, many people who had been enslaved lived in a community called the Bog.

Samuel Martin, who had been enslaved, began to live on a piece of land at the bottom of Fitzroy Street in Charlottetown that nobody else wanted, and others followed him to the area. It was called the Bog because the ground was very soft and wet. It was next to a small body of water called Government Pond. People often dumped their garbage in the pond, making the air smell really bad.

The pride of the Bog was the Bog School, which opened in 1848. The school was built for Black and white children who lived in the area. The school stayed open for more than fifty years. It wasn't long after the school closed that many people living in the Bog slowly began to find new homes elsewhere on the island.

Close to one hundred Black people lived in the Bog when it was at its peak, making it the largest Black community on Prince Edward Island. Black people in this community worked as farmers, fishers, stonecutters, and labourers. While it's no longer in existence, the Bog is an important piece of Black Islander history.

THE BLACK PIONEERS

The Black Pioneers were part of the British forces and the only all-Black regiment in the American Revolutionary War. Many had been promised freedom by Lord Dunmore, Virginia's royal governor, after the war. The call for Black enslaved people to run away from their masters to fight for the king of England was called Dunmore's Proclamation. It was announced November 7, 1775. Thousands of people risked their lives by fleeing to join the British forces. Because of the colour of their skin, they weren't allowed to fight alongside white soldiers, but performed tasks under dangerous conditions and heavy gunfire. In military terms, a "pioneer" was a soldier who would perform construction and demolition duties in camps and during combat. They cleared grounds for camps, removed debris and obstructions, and dug trenches for other (white) soldiers to advance.

In 1783, when the war was over, the Black Pioneers set sail from New York to Nova Scotia. While the **company** disbanded in Nova Scotia, it wasn't long before many of its members got to work in their new home. They, along with other Black Loyalists, helped design and build the town of Shelburne and the community of Birchtown. As promised, the men received free land, but their lots were much smaller than those given to the white soldiers. They slept in tents and small huts until their homes were built. They had nothing but boxes for beds and used furs during the winter to stay warm. Many were skilled carpenters and farmers and were employed to build some of the first communities in Nova Scotia. Their legacy lives on in areas like Birchtown, Tracadie, and the Prestons, which they established many, many years ago.

Amazing Black Atlantic Canadians

In the 1780s, Birchtown became the largest settlement of free Blacks outside Africa, with over 3,000 settlers. Birchtown, located a few kilometres south of Shelburne, Nova Scotia, was named after General Samuel Birch.

General Birch was a British officer who protected Black Loyalists in New York after the American Revolutionary War. He is also credited with signing most of the Certificates of Freedom given to enslaved Black people. In 1997, the Canadian government designated the settlement of Birchtown a National Historic Event.

BLACK LOYALIST HERITAGE CENTRE

The Black Loyalist Heritage Centre is located in Birchtown, Nova Scotia. It includes an information centre that enables visitors to follow the journey of Canada's early Black settlers. Visitors are also able to trace their own heritage and discover information about their ancestors through the centre's extensive records of names. The building's structural design represents many symbols of African-Canadian history: a pathway represents the point of no return for Africans boarding slave ships; and a large round tower was built to look like traditional African huts.

ROSE FORTUNE

ose Fortune was born in Philadelphia, Pennsylvania, in 1774 during the American Revolution. She came to Annapolis Royal, Nova Scotia, with her parents and the other Black Loyalists when she was ten years old. Rose's childhood and any information about her family is a bit of a mystery. Historians can't seem to track down information about her parents and there are no documents that tell us what it was like for Rose growing up in Nova Scotia. What we do know is that Rose eventually became a successful businesswoman and the first female police officer in Canada.

In 1825, when she was fifty-one years old, Rose started her own business. A Black woman starting her own business was unheard of at that time. Women, especially Black women, were considered inferior to white people and weren't expected to achieve much of anything in life. But that didn't stop Rose. Using a wheelbarrow, Rose would move luggage between the ferry docks and nearby homes and hotels. Rose was quick to stop any young men who tried to cut into her profits by providing the same service themselves. This role, often done by men called baggage masters, was looked down upon by many and often times people would try to steal the bags they offered to carry. The fact that people trusted Rose enough to carry their bags shows that she was respected in the community.

Her luggage-carrying business eventually included a wake-up service, where she would alert travellers at nearby inns that their ships were getting ready to depart. Because of all the time she spent at the ferry docks, Rose gradually took on the role of security guard for the wharves and warehouses, acting as Annapolis Royal's waterfront police officer. She was tough—she carried a stick as her weapon and would ward off anyone who caused trouble around the docks, and made sure everyone was following the town's nightly curfew.

Many historians consider Rose the first female police officer in Canada. Rose's business continued to grow as more and more people requested her fast and reliable service. Rose passed on her business to her grandson-in-law, Albert Lewis, and it became officially known as the Lewis Transfer Company. The wheelbarrows were eventually replaced with horse-drawn carriages. Rose's grandchildren kept the business alive until 1980, when they decided to close shop.

Rose's legacy continues to live on and inspire others. A play about her life, called *Fortune,* was written by New York playwright George Cameron Grant. In 2015, a ferry that travels between New Brunswick and Nova Scotia was named MV *Fundy Rose.* And in 2019, a permanent plaque telling Rose's story was placed on the Annapolis Royal waterfront, the same waterfront Rose walked along every day many years ago.

A watercolour painting of Rose Fortune from about 1830 is one of the only remaining paintings of a Black Loyalist, and the only known image of Rose. The picture illustrates what many people in Annapolis would see when Rose was working on the waterfront: a strong woman wearing lots of layers, a large coat, big boots, and a hat. The fact that she did not sit for the painting shows she was hardworking and always on the go.

DAVID GEORGE

avid George was the first Black Baptist preacher in Nova Scotia. He was born in Essex County, Virginia, and sailed to Halifax in 1782 with other Black Loyalists. In 1783, David moved to an area called Port Roseway, which was renamed Shelburne later that year. When he first arrived in Canada, David wasn't allowed to hold church services in the town of Shelburne, so he preached the gospel from clearings in the woods. Things changed in 1784, when a man gave David a town lot, where David built a chapel that held church services for about fifty Black people and several white people. People liked listening to David's loud and powerful voice and interesting sermons, but not everyone was happy with the new preacher in town.

On July 26, 1784, forty white Loyalists attacked and destroyed David's home with hooks and chains they had found in the harbour. Many were upset that a Black man had started a church in Shelburne and was baptizing white Loyalists. The angry mob went on to destroy twenty other homes in the area that were owned and built by Black people. This began the Shelburne Riot—the first, but sadly not last, race riot in North America. David was brave. He didn't stop preaching, so the mob returned and chased the Black preacher into a swamp. Anger grew and the riot lasted for ten days, until soldiers of the 17th regiment were called to bring peace and order.

Even though the riots had ended, Black families in Shelburne still didn't feel safe. David wanted to give people hope and comfort, so he continued to preach, sing hymns, and travel around Nova Scotia and New Brunswick. David went on to build Baptist churches all over Nova Scotia using money donated from the Black community.

Despite David's popularity, it was clear that Black families were not welcome in the Atlantic provinces and the land they had been given was small and would likely not produce many vegetables. As the weather got colder, work became even harder to come by, especially after white Loyalists protested their jobs were being taken away by the Black Loyalists.

Thomas Peters was from North Carolina and was a member of the Black Pioneers (see page 16). Like many others who had arrived in Nova Scotia after the war, Thomas was upset when he didn't receive what was promised. So, in 1790, he travelled to London to take the case of the Black Loyalists up with the British government—the very government who had promised the land in the first place. While he was overseas, Thomas learned about the Sierra Leone Company. The company was looking for Black settlers to live in their colony in West Africa.

Thomas returned to Nova Scotia to share the news that the government was offering free land in Sierra Leone and a fresh start for Black Loyalists who had been mistreated. In 1792, eight years after the Shelburne Riot, David and his family, and approximately 1,196 other Black Loyalists left Halifax on fifteen ships and sailed to Sierra Leone. They were known as the Nova Scotian Settlers. It cost the British government £15,500 (which is almost $4 million in current Canadian dollars) to complete the journey. When they arrived in Sierra Leone, they re-founded a settlement that had been previously destroyed and called it the City of Freetown, which became the capital of Sierra Leone in 1961. David founded the first Baptist church in Freetown, called Zion Church. He continued to preach right up until his death in 1810.

ELIZABETH CROMWELL

lizabeth Cromwell was determined to preserve the memories of her ancestors. When the government said they wanted to build a landfill in her community of Shelburne, she took action. Elizabeth formed the County Cultural Awareness Society in 1980, which is now known as the Black Loyalist Heritage Society. The society fought and succeeded in stopping the landfill from going forward. And this was just the beginning of the society's mission to honour and protect African Nova Scotian people and places.

Elizabeth regularly collected historical information about Black Loyalists. She loved looking through old church records and digging through library archives. The society held most of their findings in a bungalow on Old Birchtown Road. In 2006, the building was set on fire and over two decades of research about Nova Scotia's Black community was ruined. It became clear that there needed to be a new structure that was bigger and better—a place where young and old could come and find out more about their personal histories. But it was going to cost a lot of money and take a lot of time. And they needed to find a way to get all of that information back that was inside the now burnt computers.

It took almost twenty-five years to gain support from the community and surrounding areas and create a business plan. But in the end, the hard work paid off. The Black Loyalist Heritage Centre was opened in 2015. An expert with computers named David Bradley offered eighty hours of his time to get back almost all of the valuable information stored on the society's computers. Today, whether a student is looking for more information to complete a school assignment, or someone just wants to find out more about their Black heritage, they can walk through the doors of the Black Loyalist Heritage Centre and find all of the information they need at their fingertips. (See sidebar on page 17.)

Elizabeth's great knowledge of Black history was also extremely helpful for author Lawrence Hill when he was doing research for his novel, *The Book of Negroes*, which was later turned into a movie that was filmed in the Town of Shelburne.

Elizabeth was awarded the Canada 125 medal and the Queen Elizabeth Diamond Jubilee medal. In 2018, Elizabeth was honoured with the Order of Canada for helping to preserve and promote Black history in Nova Scotia.

JAMAICAN MAROONS

The British took control of Jamaica from the Spanish in 1655. During the takeover, enslaved African people escaped into the hills to form their own free community. They were called Maroons. For decades, the British battled the Maroons, trying to force them into obedience and British rule. By 1796, the British started limiting their access to food and water and using extreme force to compel the Maroons to come out of the woods. Eventually, it became too much to defend and the Maroons surrendered. Those who did not willingly surrender were forced to.

In 1796, approximately 600 men, women, and children were deported from Port Royal Harbour, Jamaica. They travelled on board British Navy transport ships that just happened to be leaving Jamaica at the same time of their deportation. The closest British port the ships would pass was Halifax, so it was decided that the Maroons would be left in Halifax until the British found a more permanent location. The majority settled in the town of Preston, where there was vacant land and farms left behind from the Black Loyalists who left in 1792. Others ended up in Sackville and Spryfield. The Maroons were inspected on the ship to ensure they were able-bodied and it was up to the government of Nova Scotia to decide what they would do once they arrived.

When the Maroons hit dry land, the provincial government put them straight to work. The English and the French were at war, and the government was concerned France would attack English-controlled Halifax. The Maroons were formed into their own militia. They were instructed to clear woods, build roads, and construct the third fortification, a building designed for military defense, to protect the city, on Citadel Hill.. They were also employed to build **Government House** alongside soldiers and white labourers.

The Maroons had escaped slavery in Jamaica, but Halifax turned out to be no better when they were forced to do hard labour for very little money. The locals didn't like how the Maroons lived and the Maroons didn't like the cold weather, deep snow, and poor crops. They were promised clothing and supplies from Britain and most things took a long time to arrive or just didn't arrive at all. To protest, the Maroons took their children out of school and refused to go to church. They sent petitions to London demanding they be relocated to a warmer climate. While many Maroons were ready to leave, others tried to adjust in Nova Scotia. A second Maroon community was created in Boydville (which is today known as Maroon Hill). They asked the government for animals and grains to try to make a living. But those who wanted to leave won in the end. By 1800, the British government arranged transport for the Maroons and about 550 Maroons set sail on board the HMS *Asia* for Freetown, Sierra Leone.

DID YOU KNOW?

To escape British attacks in Jamaica, Maroons fled to the high mountains where they would be out of sight. The word "Maroon" is derived from the Spanish word cimarron, which means runaway or wild, but to the Maroons, it meant free.

BLACK REFUGEES

fter the end of the American Revolutionary War in 1783, it didn't take long for another war to begin. The War of 1812 was between the United States and Great Britain, and brought another large migration, or movement, of Blacks to Nova Scotia. When the war first began, Blacks were not allowed to enlist. But by 1814, America needed more men and so they began enlisting Black soldiers. Many free Black men joined the navy as guides, they piloted ships, or they helped the army on raids against American forces.

The British began offering freedom to any enslaved Black person who was willing to escape their enslavers and join the opposing side. This was similar to Lord Dunmore's Proclamation during the American Revolution (see page 13). Once on board the British warships, they had the option of either serving with the British forces or becoming free settlers somewhere in North America or the West Indies. Slaves were typically used during the war as spies, sailors, labourers, and guides.

Approximately two thousand Black Refugees sailed to the Atlantic provinces by 1816. Most settled in Halifax, Dartmouth, Preston, Beechville, Beaverbank, and Hammonds Plains. Like the Black Loyalists who settled in Nova Scotia after the American Revolutionary War, the Black Refugees faced harsh conditions. The land they were given was rocky, which made it difficult to grow crops, and they faced **systemic racism** and **discrimination**. Those who were able to grow more food than others shared with their neighbours, but once winter rolled around, all were left with little or no fruits and vegetables.

In 1821, the government tried to pressure Black Refugees to leave the province and to resettle in Trinidad, but most did not want to go anywhere that still allowed people to own slaves. Approximately ninety-five Black Refugees agreed to immigrate to Trinidad, a Caribbean island near the top of South America, but the majority of the original two thousand stayed in Canada, determined to make it work.

Since their land was so poor, many Black Refugees had to make money to buy the things they could not grow. Some worked on ships or as carpenters in Halifax. Women and children went to the Saturday market and sold food, baskets, and anything else they were able to harvest or craft. They were market gardeners and seamen, and by 1834, the Black Refugees had created their own communities and become an important part of economic life in the town of Halifax.

A YEAR WITHOUT SUMMER

Many Black Refugees depended on fertile crops to survive, but the land provided by the government was rocky. In 1815, mice destroyed entire fields. And in June 1816, an unexpected ten inches of snow fell on the frozen fields, which still hadn't thawed from the winter months. It was called the "year without a summer," and the frigid conditions and ruined crops dashed any chance of producing a good harvest.

RICHARD PRESTON

ichard Preston was enslaved from his birth in Virginia in 1791. When he was a young boy, his mother was taken away from him and brought to Canada along with other Black Refugees during the War of 1812. Four years later, in 1816, Richard himself escaped slavery in Virginia and travelled to Nova Scotia. As the tale has it, Richard endured a long and difficult journey, and when he arrived in Canada, he was determined to find his mother. Tired and hungry, he knocked on the first door he saw to seek shelter for the night and to find out if his mother might be nearby. The woman who answered the door recognized a mark on the side of the weary traveller's face. To her shock and excitement, the mark looked exactly like the birthmark of her young son, whom she had not seen for many years. Miraculously, Richard and his mother were reunited the very day he arrived.

CRAIG SMITH

Craig Smith is an author, historian, and a sergeant with the Royal Canadian Mounted Police (RCMP). Craig has written many books to highlight the great achievements of Black Canadians. He also contributed to the creation of an action-packed educational video game based on the life of Reverend Richard Preston. In 2015, Craig became the first Black RCMP member to be appointed to the Order of Merit of Police Forces—an honour presented to recipients by the Governor General of Canada.

Amazing Black Atlantic Canadians

It didn't take long for Richard to leave his mark on the province and the Black community there quickly embraced him. He encouraged Black people to build their own churches, stand up to the racism they experienced, and educate their children about their heritage. He would often travel on horseback, going from town to town and preaching the gospel. And while he became well known as a preacher, he needed to be ordained to have the authority to oversee weddings, funerals, and baptisms. He would also need a chapel. Members of the community collected money to send Richard to England to become an ordained minister and to buy land to build a church.

He returned to Nova Scotia as an ordained minister and was determined to make a difference not only in the community where he was first reunited with his mother, but also in several other Black communities throughout Nova Scotia. Reverend Richard Preston founded eleven Black Baptist churches in Nova Scotia in twenty years and in 1854, he founded the African United Baptist Association. He fought for the end of slavery in Canada and the United States and his legacy continues in many of the Baptist churches that still stand today in communities across the province.

DID YOU KNOW?

The first woman to be ordained in the African United Baptist Association of Nova Scotia and the first Black ordained woman in the Canadian Baptists of Atlantic Canada was Reverend Tracey Grosse from Cherry Brook, Nova Scotia, in 1996.

PART II

ATHLETES

" *You can do whatever you want to do,*
you just have to want to do it. "

—Marjorie Turner-Bailey, sprinter

" *We're here to participate. We're here*
to play and enjoy, but never forget
you're here to represent the Island. "

—Charlie Ryan, baseball

ATHLETES

**B**lack Atlantic Canadian athletes have a long history of overcoming racism and discrimination to achieve their goals. Despite their talent, Black hockey players, boxers, runners, and more were told they were not allowed to compete alongside other athletes—simply because of the colour of their skin. Not allowing Black athletes to compete in professional sports was called the **colour barrier**.

Professional American baseball player Jackie Robinson was one of the first athletes to break the colour barrier, in 1945. From rookie of the year to an all-star several times over, Jackie accomplished greatness in his sport and became a hero on and off the field. Just like Jackie, the amazing athletes on these pages have reached the top of their sport not only in the Atlantic provinces, but also in Canada and around the world. They are trailblazers who have paved the way for future athletes and have proudly put their hometowns on the map.

While their athletic achievements are incredible in themselves, it is their courage and determination to beat all odds to follow their dreams that make these individuals truly amazing.

GEORGE DIXON

George Dixon was born in 1870 in Africville, Nova Scotia. When he was a young boy, he worked as an apprentice with a photographer. He first took an interest in boxing after seeing several local boxers come into the studio to sit for photographs. In 1886, when George was sixteen years old, he made his boxing debut in Boston, Massachusetts. George weighed only 87 pounds and stood just 5'3.5" tall. Promoters gave him the nickname "Little Chocolate"—they assumed because of his size and skin colour, he wouldn't be a real contender in the ring. But George proved everyone wrong and went on to become one of the greatest boxers of all time.

George accomplished a number of firsts during his boxing career, including being named the world boxing champion—twice! In 1888, George won his first world boxing championship in the eighteenth round as a bantamweight, making him the first ever Black man and first ever Canadian world boxing champion of any origin or weight class.

A typical boxing match has twelve rounds and each round is three minutes long. But in 1891, after he had gained a bit of weight, George fought and beat boxer Cal MacCarthy after a gruelling twenty-two rounds, making him the world featherweight champion.

George is credited for developing the art of shadowboxing, which means to fight against an invisible opponent as a training technique. George was also recorded as being the first person to use a punching bag suspended from the ceiling. He was inducted into Canada's Sports Hall of Fame in 1955, and the International Boxing Hall of Fame as a first-class inductee in 1990. In 2018, George was named one of the greatest fifteen athletes in Nova Scotia's history. The George Dixon Community Recreation Centre located in Halifax's North End was built to honour his great legacy.

AFRICVILLE

fricville is located on the southern shore of the Bedford Basin in North End Halifax. Black settlers founded the community in 1749. Residents of Africville caught and sold fish fresh from the Bedford Basin, picked wild berries to sell at local markets, tended to farms, and owned small stores. Even though they paid taxes just like everyone else in Halifax, they were denied basic city services, like running water and paved roads.

In 1849, the community opened Seaview African United Baptist Church. The church was the heart of the community and held all kinds of events, like weddings and baptisms.

In 1854, a railway was built right through the middle of Africville. Some homes were destroyed to build the tracks, and the trains brought pollution and noise into the village. The City of Halifax also added a fertilizer plant, a prison, and a garbage dump. Beautiful Africville was being destroyed and its people were fighting to save their beloved home.

The Halifax Explosion of 1917 destroyed most of Africville. While millions of dollars were donated to help to rebuild the city after the explosion, not a penny went to rebuilding Africville. But the people of Africville were still resilient and took great pride in their community.

In the 1960s, Halifax City Council voted to move Africville residents to another part of the city, without consulting the residents themselves. Council decided to tear down all the homes, farms, churches, and businesses on the land. For five years, the people of Africville who fought so hard to stay had to watch each home be bulldozed to the ground. The residents and all of their things were moved out in garbage trucks. The city promised to provide better housing for Africville's evicted residents elsewhere in Halifax, but that promise was never kept. Some families were moved into housing projects in run-down parts of Halifax, and others were sent further away from the city to areas like

Hammonds Plains. A close community was now scattered all over the city and that feeling of support and togetherness was gone. Many had to deal with racism when their new white neighbours complained about having to live next to Black families. Jobs were hard to find when no one wanted to hire a Black man or woman and many had to turn to welfare because living in the city was more expensive. In 1969, the last property was destroyed and Africville's 400 residents were all gone.

If you visit Africville today, you'll find a grassy park, which was renamed Africville Park. The church, which was torn down in the middle of the night, was rebuilt as a church museum in 2012 to commemorate a once vibrant community.

The people of Africville now bring their children, grandchildren, and great-grandchildren to visit the park for picnics in the summer and church services at Christmastime. Their houses may have been destroyed, but their memories will never be forgotten.

DID YOU KNOW?

In 1970, evicted Africville resident Eddie Carvery returned to Africville and pitched a tent in protest of losing his land. He has lived there in trailers off and on for more than forty years since the community was destroyed. It earned him the nickname the Hermit of Africville. In 2010, the mayor of Halifax gave a public apology for taking the land from the people of Africville. But Eddie, who is now in his seventies, wants the city to allow residents to return to their rightful home, or compensate them for the loss of their land. And he's determined to stay in his trailer, on the land he calls home, for as long as that takes.

SAM LANGFORD

lack Loyalists and their descendants have done some pretty amazing things to create a lasting legacy in the Atlantic provinces, and one of the greatest boxers of all time is on that list.

Sam Langford left home when he was just a teenager. He was born in Weymouth Falls in 1886, which was a small community in Nova Scotia settled by Black Loyalists and formerly enslaved people, like Sam's grandfather, William.

After Sam's mother died when he was just twelve years old, he left home and started doing odd jobs to support himself. He worked as a logger and ox-driver in Nova Scotia, and was a cabin boy on a ship. He travelled to New Hampshire, New England, and worked on a farm, but he was fired for fighting with other men who also worked on the farm. Sam went on to Boston, Massachusetts. He walked the whole way there and worked at different brick and lumber yards on his journey to make a bit of money. When he finally got to Boston, he found a job as a janitor at the Lenox Athletic Club—a gym for local boxers. When he wasn't cleaning, Sam would spar with boxers who trained at the club. The club's owner, Joe Woodman, was impressed by Sam's skills. He offered to be his manager and that began Sam's twenty-four-year boxing career.

Sam picked up the sport quickly and despite being only 5'7", he found great success against opponents who were much larger than he was. In 1901, when he was just fifteen years old, Sam won the amateur featherweight championship of Boston. In 1902, when he was sixteen years old, he won his first professional fight in a knockout victory. Eighteen months later, Sam had his first shot at winning a title. On December 8, 1903, he beat out lightweight division champion and the first African-American to win a world championship, Joe Gans, in fifteen rounds. But because it was discovered that Sam weighed a little more than 135 pounds, he was not awarded the belt. Sam held the heavyweight championships of England, Spain, and Mexico, and was considered the best fighter never to win a title in the United States.

Sam faced several racial barriers throughout his boxing career. Promoters didn't think a white audience would pay to watch two Black boxers compete and white boxing champions refused to fight Sam out of fear of losing their belts.

During a fight in 1917, Sam lost the vision in his left eye. But that didn't stop him from boxing. For the next eight years, Sam continued to fight professionally with the help of someone guiding him into the ring. His final fight was scheduled in 1926, but it had to be cancelled because he couldn't see his opponent.

Between 1906 and 1914, Sam won eighty-five of eighty-seven fights. He was inducted into Canada's Sports Hall of Fame, the International Boxing Hall of Fame, and the Nova Scotia Sport Hall of Fame. In 1955, Sam became the first boxer voted into the Boxing Hall of Fame without ever winning a world championship. In 1999, Sam was named Nova Scotia's top male athlete of the twentieth century.

There is a proud history of Black Atlantic Canadians rising up in the boxing world and making a name for themselves on the international stage. Today's boxers can thank people like George Dixon and Sam Langford for breaking down barriers to ensure they can also do what they love.

CUSTIO CLAYTON

Custio Clayton's path to become a professional boxer began at his great-uncle's gym, City of Lakes Boxing Club, in Dartmouth, Nova Scotia. Custio fought his first amateur fight when he was just eleven years old. In 2018, he was ranked No. 1 in the World Boxing Organization rankings. He is a six-time Canadian amateur boxing champion and represented Canada at the 2012 Olympics in London, England.

KIRK JOHNSON

Kirk Johnson was born in North Preston, Nova Scotia. Kirk represented Canada at the 1992 Summer Olympics in Barcelona, Catalonia, Spain. He lost his bout in the quarter-final round. Kirk has an impressive amateur record of seventy-six wins and only seven losses.

MARJORIE TURNER-BAILEY

arjorie Turner-Bailey was born in 1947 and grew up in the small fishing village of Lockeport, Nova Scotia. Her mother and father were descendants of Black Loyalists who had settled in the Shelburne area in 1783. Marjorie loved being outside and playing sports. She excelled on her high school soccer team and was the star of the Lockeport High School women's basketball team. But there was one particular sport that earned Marjorie national attention.

Marjorie's gym teacher first noticed her amazing potential as a track and field athlete and entered Marjorie's high school track team into the Mount Allison Relays in 1964. Marjorie won all of the running events and all of the field events. While some thought she had taken home the top prizes by chance and not skill, they were quickly proven wrong when she entered the biggest track and field event in Nova Scotia later that year, called the Acadia Relays. Once again, Marjorie won all of the running events, the javelin, and discus.

Marjorie was quick on her feet. She ran the 100-yard dash in 11.1 seconds and the 220-yard in 24.7 seconds. At just sixteen years old, Marjorie was named Nova Scotia Athlete of the Year. Marjorie trained hard and was always looking to improve. Her hard work paid off when she attended the Canadian Olympic Time Trials in St. Lambert, Quebec. She ran the 100 metres in twelve seconds flat, putting her in second place and qualifying for the 1964 Tokyo Olympics when she was sixteen years old.

Unfortunately, an injury prevented her from competing, but Marjorie didn't let the setback stop her. In 1972, Marjorie set her sights on the Munich Olympics. She woke up at 3:30 A.M. every morning and had to squeeze in her training while balancing two jobs to support herself and her son. Although she didn't qualify for the Munich Olympics, Marjorie made headlines the following year when she won a race at the 1973 Vancouver Relays. After almost six years away from competition, Marjorie amazed crowds when she completed the 100-metre in 11.7 seconds.

Marjorie continued her training by competing in track meets all over the world, including Switzerland, England, Denmark, and Sweden. In 1976, at twenty-eight years old, Marjorie's goal of Olympic competition finally came to be when she qualified for the 100, 200, the 4x100 relay, and as an alternate for the 4x400 relay for the Montreal Olympics. Marjorie made the semi-finals in both the 100 and 200 metres. She made eight Olympic appearances in three different events and she and her teammates set a Canadian record in the 4x100 relay. In 1978, Marjorie won a silver medal at the 1978 Commonwealth Games in Edmonton.

Despite many roadblocks along the way, Marjorie never stopped working towards her dreams and is an inspiration for all athletes to never give up.

WILLIE O'REE

Fourteen-year-old Willie O'Ree from Fredericton, New Brunswick, was a pretty good baseball player. When his team won their league championship in 1949, they were treated to a trip to New York City. The highlight of the trip was a Dodgers baseball game. Two years earlier, Jackie Robinson broke the colour barrier in baseball and joined the majors. Willie got to meet Jackie at that game, telling him, "I'm a baseball player, but what I really love is hockey."

And Willie turned out to be a pretty good hockey player too. In 1958, he was in his second season playing for the Quebec Aces in the Quebec Senior Hockey League. The Boston Bruins were looking for someone to replace one of their injured players and they called Willie. Willie's talent on the ice impressed the Bruins, and he was ready and eager to play. He accepted the invitation, and conveniently left out one important piece of information: he could only see out of one eye.

Two years earlier, Willie had been hit in the right eye with a wayward hockey puck and lost 95 percent of the vision in his right eye. Only his sister and a good friend knew of the injury; Willie had decided to keep it a secret because he knew teams wouldn't want him. To make up for the injury, Willie played left wing and perfected a left-handed shot.

On January 18, 1958, just as Jackie Robinson did years before him, Willie crossed the National Hockey League's colour line and became the first Black player in the league. The Boston Bruins were playing the Montreal Canadiens, a team Willie grew up watching. The Bruins won that game 3–0 and then headed back to Boston. On home turf, they lost the second game against the Canadiens

5–3. Willie only played two games that season, but in 1960 he had his second opportunity to play for the Bruins. This time, Willie played forty-three games, earning fourteen points on four goals and ten assists.

While Willie focused on the game, his opponents often focused on the colour of his skin. He was often targeted with cheap shots and racist slurs, but that didn't stop him from giving his all on the ice. The media called Willie "the Jackie Robinson of hockey." Once the 1960 season was over, Willie returned to the minors and that is where he finished his professional career, playing in the Western Hockey League for teams in Los Angeles and San Diego.

Willie retired in 1979. In 1984, he was inducted into the New Brunswick Sports Hall of Fame. In 1998, Willie became the director of youth development for the NHL. He wanted to encourage young people, just like that fourteen-year old boy who played baseball but loved hockey, to learn how to play the game.

In 2005, the Fredericton Arena was renamed Willie O'Ree Place. While Willie received many honours in his life, perhaps one of the most memorable was in 1962. Willie was twenty-seven when he attended an event in Los Angeles. At the event, he came face to face with Jackie Robinson, but this time he didn't have to introduce himself. "You're the young fellow I met in Brooklyn," said Jackie. Greatness recognized greatness, and Willie O'Ree paved the way for many more Black hockey players to enter the game and do what they love.

JOHN PARIS JR.

John Paris Jr. grew up in Currys Corner in Windsor, Nova Scotia. As a young boy, John loved sports—especially baseball and hockey. John loved the details behind sports and the strategy. He and his friends would watch the older kids playing hockey and would clear a small patch of ice on the outdoor pond and try to mimic their moves.

When John was outside with his friends one day, his brother Percy came running towards them to tell John that a Montreal Canadiens scout, Scotty Bowman, was waiting in their parents' living room. He wanted to talk to John. When he was seventeen years old, John travelled to Montreal and tried out for the Junior Canadiens. He didn't make the team, but this was the beginning of John's hockey career as a player, scout, and coach. The next season he played for the Maisonneuve Braves in the Metropolitan Montreal Junior Hockey League. At the time, John was rated one of the top junior prospects in eastern Canada. People called him the "Chocolate Rocket" because of how fast he was on the ice.

Despite his clear skill, John faced a lot of racism and discrimination during his time in the junior hockey league in the 1960s. He and his family were called names and received threats, and he was bullied on and off the ice. John had heard these taunts since he was a young boy playing baseball in Currys Corner when he got booed during an away game. His dad wanted him to know those unkind words should be his motivation to succeed. "He said, 'Son, it's because you're good at what you're doing. You start worrying when they do not notice you. You're doing things other kids cannot do at your age. You have to expect that. You need to use that as motivation. The day you do not hear a sound, you start asking yourself questions.'" In 1967, John became the first Black player in the Southern Division of the Eastern Hockey League. He played nine games during the 1967–68 season for the Knoxville Knights.

After that ninth game, John started to feel really sick. He was tired, his body hurt, and his temperature went from hot to cold in seconds. John was diagnosed with Hodgkin's lymphoma, a type of cancer that begins in the white blood cells. His time as a player was cut short, but his career in the hockey world was far from over.

After his time as a junior hockey player, John worked as a scout and a coach. He became the first Black coach to lead a professional hockey team to a championship when he coached the Atlanta Knights to the Turner Cup in 1994 in the International Hockey League. The city of Atlanta held a large parade to celebrate their champions. Streets were closed and the players, coaches, firetrucks, and the team's Zamboni made their way past the cheering crowd. In 2005, John was inducted into the Nova Scotia Sport Hall of Fame.

ELDRIDGE (GUS) EATMAN

In 1905, Eldridge (Gus) Eatman became the fastest man in the world. Anyone would be excited to have this title, but it was even more amazing for Gus because at the time, Black people were fighting to be accepted and respected as track and field athletes. Gus was determined to overcome racism and poverty to compete.

Gus was born near Fredericton in 1880, but lived most of his life in Saint John. He started his career as a sprinter in 1903 when he beat world champion 120-yard sprinter Tom Keen at Moosepath in Saint John. Two years later at the Maritime championship, Gus clocked 9.8 seconds in the 100-yard sprint, making him, for a time, the fastest man in the world. From 1904 to 1907, he became the world professional sprint champion and made running waves in North America and Europe. In 1915, after an impressive career on the track, Gus fought on the front lines with a British regiment in the First World War, spending 785 days in the trenches. In 2002, Gus was inducted into the Saint John Sports Hall of Fame and the New Brunswick Sports Hall of Fame in 2016. In 2019, Gus's name was also added to the Maritime Sport Hall of Fame.

ROCKY JOHNSON (WADE DOUGLAS BOWLES)

Dwayne (The Rock) Johnson always mentions his dad, Rocky Johnson, when he talks about his role models and mentors. After all, it was his dad who first showed him the ropes in the wrestling world. As a young boy, Dwayne would sit in the stands and watch in amazement as his father put on a show for his fans. Of course, with his dad as his inspiration, Dwayne went on to become one of the most popular wrestlers in the world, before becoming a famous actor and producer. He always thanks his dad for inspiring him, but the road to success wasn't easy for Rocky.

Rocky's father passed away when he was just twelve years old, and at fourteen years of age, he left home with a few dollars, a suitcase, and great determination to make a life for himself. Rocky moved to Toronto and worked as a truck driver and eventually discovered his love for wrestling. He knew little about the sport up until that point, so he enrolled in a wrestling school in Hamilton, Ontario, to learn more.

In 1965, he changed his name from Wade Douglas Bowles to Rocky Johnson to become a professional wrestler. Rocky loved getting into the ring and he spent hours studying and trying to improve his craft. Over the course of a thirty-year career, he held fifty-six different titles and became the first Black man to win Southern, Georgia, and Florida heavyweight titles. He was also part of the first Black tag team, called "The Soul Patrol," who won the World Tag Team Championship for the World Wrestling Federation.

Amazing Black Atlantic Canadians

Rocky had fans all over the world, and on a particular tour to Saudi Arabia he was lowered into a soccer stadium by helicopter because he couldn't walk his way through the 100,000-plus screaming fans. Rocky fought through several injuries throughout the years, but when his shoulder and knee started to become more of an issue in his late forties, he decided it was time to step out of the ring. Throughout his career, Rocky sparred with boxing greats such as Mohammed Ali and George Foreman, and went on to be inducted into the World Wrestling Entertainment Hall of Fame.

It's no wonder Dwyane was so inspired by his dad. Rocky wasn't just his dad; he was his hero.

CHRIS SKINNER

Chris Skinner started playing football when he was twelve years old. When he was fourteen, Chris was voted rookie of the year in the New Brunswick High School Football League. In 1983, Chris played for Bishop's University in Lennoxville, Quebec, and finished the season with the most rushes in the league. He earned a spot on the all-star team and was voted outstanding player in the Ontario-Quebec conference.

The Canadian Football League had started to take notice of Chris and they were impressed by what they saw. In 1984, Chris was selected seventh overall in the CFL by the Edmonton Eskimos. Chris played five seasons with Edmonton and became a starter in 1986. He was nominated as the league's most outstanding player. The next year, in 1987, Edmonton beat the Toronto Argonauts 38-36 to become Grey Cup champions. Chris led his team's running backs with 889 total yards for the season. In 1989, Chris was traded to the Ottawa Rough Riders and stayed there for one season before going to the British Columbia Lions in 1990.

Chris was now a veteran in the league, and the Lions looked to him to be a mentor to the younger players. Chris retired with the Lions in 1993. He finished his career with 24 touchdowns, 2,850 yards rushing and 2,874 yards on pass receptions. Chris was elected to the Saint John Sports Hall of Fame in 1997, and the New Brunswick Sports Hall of Fame in 2003.

DELMORE WILLIAM "BUDDY" DAYE

hen Delmore William "Buddy" Daye was five years old, he was brought to Halifax from New Glasgow, where he was raised by foster parents. When he was a teenager, Buddy worked as a merchant marine and travelled around the world. Buddy also worked as a railroad porter and eventually found his way to a successful career in boxing.

His first fight was sensational: it was May of 1995, and Buddy won the bout after just twenty-one seconds! Fans loved watching Buddy and his quick punch, and Buddy genuinely loved boxing. He fought several times a month and promoters were eager to have Buddy face off against lots of different opponents to showcase his skill. He was light on his feet; he moved swiftly around the ring, and was hard to tire. Over his career, Buddy fought 88 fights—and won 81 of them. Of those wins, 77 were knockout victories.

It wasn't all glory, of course. There were plenty of times Buddy and other Black boxers faced racism in Halifax gyms. In response, they built their own gym on Creighton Street in the city's North End. In 1964, Buddy won the Canadian Junior Lightweight title in front of five thousand cheering fans at the Halifax Forum. In 1981, he was inducted into the Nova Scotia Sport Hall of Fame.

When not in the ring, Buddy was a community activist and worked to improve employment and living conditions for Black Nova Scotians. He worked with young people in his community and helped many get their first jobs. On January 1, 1990, Buddy became the first Black Nova Scotian sergeant-at-arms, an officer who maintains order and security, for the Nova Scotia House of Assembly. In 1996, a photograph was permanently placed in the

Nova Scotia House of Assembly to honour his memory. In 2006, Gerrish Street in Halifax was renamed Buddy Daye Street. But perhaps Buddy's biggest legacy is the lessons he shared with his nine children. Buddy taught his children that one man or woman can do so much and there is still work to be done to make the world a better place for all ages and races.

THE DELMORE "BUDDY" DAYE LEARNING INSTITUTE

The Delmore "Buddy" Daye Learning Institute opened its doors in 2012. The institute is a hub of activity and, among other things, its staff works hard to organize workshops for the African Nova Scotian community, to create fun and educational contests about Black history for schoolchildren, and hold an awards ceremony called the Ancestral Roots Awards: Celebrating Young Adult Leaders. The awards are given to young men and women who are making a difference in their communities. Making sure Black youth get as many opportunities as possible was important to Buddy. He would have been pretty proud to know his name lives on and his legacy and work continues today thanks to the Delmore "Buddy" Daye Learning Institute.

GEORGE GODFREY

George Godfrey's first fights didn't happen in the boxing ring. They happened in the school yard in his hometown of Charlottetown, Prince Edward Island. George was born in 1853 and lived in the Bog, a part of Charlottetown's west end (see page 15). Growing up, George was bullied because he was Black. He fought all the time and quickly learned how to defend himself against people who tried to give him a hard time. George received his first real boxing lesson at the Richmond Street boxing academy, which was run by another Black boxer named Dick Cronin.

Like many young men at that time who were in search of bigger and better opportunities, George left the Island when he was eighteen years old and found work as a custodian at a silk factory in Boston. When he wasn't working, George took boxing classes at Professor Bailey's Hub City Gym. At twenty-seven years old—considered rather old to start prizefighting—George made his professional boxing debut and out-punched veteran boxer Professor Hadley in a six-round bout. Thanks to his hard work and powerful right hand, George became the first US coloured heavyweight champion.

Known as "Old Chocolate," George tried for several years to spar against John L. Sullivan, also known as "The Boston Strong Boy." John refused to fight George in fear of losing to a Black boxer, but in 1881, so the tale goes, the two met at the Bailey Gym only to be stopped by police right before getting into the ring because boxing was against the law at that time in the state of Massachusetts.

George wanted to fight white boxers and he knew until that was possible, he wouldn't be given the title of world champion; he would always be the "coloured" world heavyweight champion. But the best white boxers didn't want to risk losing their title to a skilled Black boxer like George.

Even though most of his opponents were up to twenty pounds heavier than he was, George racked up about one hundred bouts throughout his career. On August 24, 1888, George fought Australia's legendary Black champion Peter Jackson. Peter weighed in at 195 pounds to George's 175, and went on to defeat George after nineteen rounds.

George boxed into his forties and retired from active competition in 1895. But that doesn't mean he hung up his gloves completely. George ran a boxing school in Boston which trained many boxers who went on to be champions. He returned to PEI in 1899 for a boxing exhibition that drew many locals who were eager to get a glimpse of the hometown hero. George died when he was only forty-eight years old from an illness called tuberculosis. He was inducted into the PEI Sports Hall of Fame on June 24, 1990.

GEORGE "BUDGE" BYERS

George Godfrey's legacy lives on through several notable Black Atlantic Canadian boxers, some of whom also hailed from the Bog in PEI and were inspired by George's success. This includes George "Budge" Byers, who was born in 1872.

Just like George Godfrey, George Byers also left Charlottetown to find work. Byers started wrestling, and during one of his fights, he met Godfrey. Godfrey trained Byers to become a boxer. He fought over 125 professional fights from 1895 to 1904 and in those first four years he never lost a battle. He earned the nickname "Budge" because when he was hit, he barely moved—he stood strong, took the hit, and kept fighting. Like his trainer and mentor, Byers also won the coloured middleweight and heavyweight world titles.

When Byers retired in 1904, he began training other up-and-coming boxers. This includes another amazing Black Atlantic Canadian by the name of Sam Langford (see page 36).

WAYNE SMITH

s a boy in the 1950s, Wayne Smith loved running around the fields in Halifax with his friends, playing basketball at the local YMCA, going swimming in the ocean, and fishing off the wharf. He preferred basketball to football and didn't really consider pursuing football until he was eighteen years old and saw his brother play. Wayne didn't play football for his high school or in college. When he was a teenager in the late 1960s, he played for a senior football team called the Halifax Buccaneers. The Buccaneers played exhibition games against universities and military teams. Wayne played against men who were much older than him, and his ability to not only keep up but stand out against these seasoned athletes earned him the attention of scouts for the Canadian Football League (CFL).

The Montreal Alouettes and the Ottawa Rough Riders were both interested in having Wayne play for them. When he was nineteen years old, Wayne decided to move to Ottawa. Because he didn't have that much experience playing football, Wayne had to learn quickly and put in a lot of hard work to become a better player. He watched the professional football players on television and imagined what he would do if he were on the field.

Wayne was a tough player who was quick on his feet. In his first season as a Rough Rider, just two months before his twentieth birthday, his team won the CFL's championship trophy, the Grey Cup. Four years later, in 1973, Wayne and the Rough Riders won the cup again, this time against the Edmonton Eskimos. That season, Wayne broke his arm and ended up playing the championship game wearing a cast protected by layers of sponge and rubber. Talk about tough!

Wayne played in the CFL for twelve years on five different teams. He was named a defensive all-star while playing with the Ottawa Rough Riders. In 1974, Wayne was runner-up for the Schenley Award as the CFL's top defensive player. In 1984, Wayne was inducted into the Nova Scotia Sport Hall of Fame.

**W**ayne is not the only Black Nova Scotian who left a mark on the football world. Nova Scotia has been proudly represented in the CFL and the NFL by a few other talented Atlantic Canadians.

TYRONE WILLIAMS

In high school in Halifax, Tyrone Williams played competitive football, soccer, and basketball. In football, he excelled as an all-star as both a quarterback and wide receiver. Tyrone became the first player to win the Vanier Cup (for Canadian university football), the Super Bowl, and the Grey Cup. He was inducted into the Nova Scotia Sport Hall of Fame in 2004.

DWAYNE PROVO

The Saskatchewan Roughriders drafted North Preston's Dwayne Provo in 1995. He played in the CFL for eight years and had one season in the National Football League (NFL) with the New England Patriots.

REGGIE BOUDREAU

Reggie Boudreau says football kept him out of trouble when he was growing up in Truro. He played in the CFL for the Saskatchewan Roughriders and the Hamilton Tiger-Cats in 1979. In 1986, Reggie was inducted into the Saskatchewan Sports Hall of Fame.

JUSTINE COLLEY-LEGER

Justine Colley-Leger can remember going door-to-door in East Preston when she was just eight years old to raise money for basketball tournaments. East Preston is where she grew up and her community always wanted to help her achieve her goals and help her pursue her love of the game.

While earning a degree in finance, Justine played basketball for the Saint Mary's University Huskies for five years. In one season, she scored 565 points—the most any Atlantic university player has ever scored in one season. After five seasons, Justine scored a total of 2,376 points. This is more points than any other women's basketball player in Canadian university sports history! Justine helped lead her team to four straight conference championships and was named the player of the year twice at the university level. In 2019, she was inducted into the Nova Scotia Sport Hall of Fame.

While Justine could have pursued a professional career in basketball that would've taken her to the Olympics or the Women's National Basketball Association, she wanted a life beyond basketball. Justine wanted to start a family of her own and help her hometown community to thrive. Off the court, Justine fights for basic human rights for the residents of East Preston, like clean drinking water. She also works to help bring different communities—that, for the most part, have always been seen as separate—together.

CHARLIE RYAN

s a young boy growing up in the west end of Charlottetown, Prince Edward Island, Charlie Ryan loved playing sports with his friends. From badminton and wrestling, to kick the can, Charlie was a natural athlete. But his real gift was baseball. He could play every position on the field and was the star of the Canadiens, a junior baseball team in Charlottetown.

When the Second World War broke out in 1939, Charlie joined the army and travelled to Camp Aldershot in Kentville, Nova Scotia, to train with the other troops. And when he wasn't training, Charlie was playing baseball. After twenty-mile marches with his troop during the day, Charlie would then hike another ten miles that evening to practise with the Kentville baseball team called the Junior Wildcats. He also played for the Canadian Army Baseball Team.

After returning from the war, Charlie continued playing baseball and was an all-star catcher and pitcher. One of his greatest baseball accomplishments was when he was chosen to play one game against an American League team. Charlie got to be on the same field as some of the best players in the major league, including hall-of-famer Hank Greenberg of the Detroit Tigers.

In 1946, Charlie lead the City League All-Stars to a Maritime baseball title after they beat the Sydney Mines. It was the first championship ever won by a Prince Edward Island baseball team. That same year, Charlie began teaching younger baseball teams. Kids looked up to Charlie and he was a leader in his community. In 1949, the Charlottetown All-stars became Maritime champions once again.

Charlie did get another taste of major league baseball when he was hired as a regional scout for the Toronto Blue Jays. His job was to find young and talented players to join the professional team. In 1986, Charlie organized a Charlottetown baseball league, which was later named the Charlie Ryan Baseball League to honour his memory. It's no wonder that on Prince Edward Island, Charlie is lovingly known as "Mister Baseball."

THE COLORED HOCKEY LEAGUE

There was a time in professional hockey when things like slapshots or goaltenders dropping to their knees to cover the puck were prohibited. Today's hockey greats can thank the Colored Hockey League for revolutionizing the game.

The Colored Hockey League (CHL) was an all-Black men's hockey league founded in 1895 in Halifax, Nova Scotia. The league was started as a way to get young men to attend Sunday church services. After Sunday's service, the men would head to the ice and play against other church teams from the community. At the beginning, the league featured only three teams, including the Dartmouth Jubilees. But it quickly grew to include players from across the Maritimes playing for teams like the Africville Seasides, the Truro Victorias, the Amherst Royals, and the Charlottetown West End Rangers.

CHL players were permitted access to the arenas after the whites-only leagues had finished their seasons, which meant the CHL typically ran their games between late January and early

DID YOU KNOW?
North Preston has the largest population of African Canadians per capita across Canada. The community can trace its origins back to Black Loyalists, the Maroons, and the Black Refugees.

Amazing Black Atlantic Canadians

March. Eight short weeks of play meant only the top three or four teams would play a handful of games each to determine the champion.

The league had no official rule book, and would reference the Bible when a tough decision needed to be made. But no rules also meant it was a faster and more physical game, and CHL players quickly developed their own style of hockey, which would revolutionize professional play decades later. By 1900, the Colored Hockey League was bringing in more fans than the whites-only leagues throughout Nova Scotia. On February 18, 1902, twelve thousand people packed a Halifax arena to witness the first Inter-provincial Maritime Championship between the Africville Seasides and the Charlottetown West End Rangers. It was a close battle, but the Seasides won the game 3–2.

At the start of the twentieth century, provincial and city officials in Halifax wanted to build a new railway track that would run right through the heart of the historic Black community of Africville. The track would split Africville in two and some homes would be destroyed to make room for the railway. James Robinson Johnston was the CHL's organizer and he represented members of Africville as they fought against this new plan. Because of the legal battle, some rink owners refused to rent out their ice to the league—or to any Black hockey teams for that matter. Other rink owners would only rent their rinks in late March, when the ice was beginning to melt. Local newspapers stopped covering CHL games, and with poor or no ice to play on and no one promoting the games, the league was forced to go back to playing on local frozen ponds.

But in 1921, the league reappeared with three teams: the Truro Victorias, the Africville Seasides, and the Halifax All-Stars. The Truro and Halifax teams featured a new generation of players, while the Africville Seasides' lineup was almost identical to its original team. This time around, the league followed standardized hockey rules. Even though more teams emerged—like the Halifax Diamonds, the New Glasgow Speed Boys, and the Truro Sheiks—people eventually lost interest in regional leagues, turning their attention to the growing National Hockey League. Sadly, the CHL and its players became a thing of the past by the outbreak of the Second World War.

PART III

ARTISTS

"*Keep on being a star in your own right. Keep on defining yourself. Don't be defined by others.*"

–George Elliott Clarke, poet and playwright

"*Nobody ever told me to sing, I was born singing. I think that if nobody had ever talked to me, I wouldn't be able to communicate in any other way but by singing. I was always bowing in my dreams and singing before people and parading across the stage as a very little girl.*"

–Portia White, contralto

ARTISTS

tlantic Canada is bursting at the seams with Black artistic talent and creativity. Amazing artists have used their pens, paintbrushes, hands, musical instruments, or voices to tell stories and create beauty. Through their craft, they've shared joy and pain. Often, their art tells the artist's own personal story, or the story of their ancestors who came to Atlantic Canada by boat as Black Loyalists, Black Refugees, or Jamaican Maroons. We can learn so much just by listening to, watching, or reading their words. Beauty comes in so many different forms and art is interpreted in so many different ways. An upbeat song may make you tap your toe; a poem about the sun, the moon, and the stars may make you smile; and a book written by a young girl filled with imagination and wonder might inspire you to dream big and reach for the stars. That is the power of the artist and that is what makes their craft truly amazing.

WALTER BORDEN

hen Walter Borden was ten years old, he knew he wanted to be an actor. His first time on stage was during a Christmas play when he was in Grade 6 in New Glasgow. But before he would fully commit to his passion as an actor, he studied to become a teacher. During his first year as a teacher, Walter went to Cornwallis Street Baptist Church in Halifax to hear a man named Rocky Jones speak, and he was inspired. In his classroom, Walter taught his students all about the civil rights movement and Black history—the same topics Rocky was preaching about. Walter was eager to get more involved. He worked with Rocky and Rocky's wife, Joan, on several community projects, including Kwacha House, a club in Halifax where youth of all races could come to talk about discrimination,

education, housing, and much more. He also worked for a Nova Scotia organization called the Black United Front, which published a monthly magazine. Walter was in charge of putting the publication together and filled the pages with articles and photos of different civil rights activists and talked about the work they were doing in their own communities.

Although Walter loved to teach, the stage was calling his name. So he left the classroom and travelled to New York City in 1967 to study at the Circle in the Square Theatre School and the Herbert Beghof Studio. Three years later, Walter returned to Halifax. He joined Halifax's Neptune Theatre company in 1972.

Walter has captivated audiences across Canada and has starred in many Canadian theatre, film, and television productions. He's

DID YOU KNOW?

Walter Borden performed in a play called Whylah Falls, *written by Nova Scotian author George Elliott Clarke. The two first met when they performed together in a 1976 Christmas production of* Puss in Boots *in Halifax. Walter played the lead role of Puss, and George played a character named Cedric, who was the king's servant. Walter is a poet as well as an actor, and George was in awe of Walter's great ability to excel at both crafts. George, now an acclaimed poet himself, says Walter was his greatest and most important mentor.*

performed in several Shakespeare plays, including *Hamlet* and *A Midsummer Night's Dream*. He wrote and performed in a one-man show called *The Epistle of Tightrope Time*, which follows a Black gay man who was raised in rural Nova Scotia and the many difficulties he faced, including racism, poverty, and homophobia. It started as a book about his life that he began writing in 1974.

In 2019, at the age of seventy-seven years old, for the first time in his acting career, Walter was cast in a part that reflects his Black-Indigenous identity. The play was based on a movie called *Lillies*, and Walter played a Métis man in a Quebec jail named Simon. Walter was proud to represent his Métis heritage.

Walter has been honoured with the Queen Elizabeth II Golden Jubilee Medal, the Order of Canada, the Order of Nova Scotia, and the Martin Luther King Jr. Achievement Award.

MEASHA BRUEGGERGOSMAN

easha Brueggergosman is a soprano opera singer. Her stunning voice has captivated audiences around the world. And it all began in her hometown of Fredericton, New Brunswick. As a young girl, Measha sang in the choir of her local Baptist church and studied piano and voice with the church's choir director. Those who heard Measha sing knew she had a gift and the people in her hometown wanted to make sure she had everything she needed to master her craft.

While attending the University of Toronto for her Bachelor of Music, Measha would come home to Fredericton once a year to perform a concert. The proceeds from the concerts helped pay for her education. Measha spent her summers studying at the Boston Conservatory and also spent time training and studying for her Masters degree in Düsseldorf, Germany.

When she was twenty years old, Measha took the lead role in an opera called *Beatrice Chancy*. The opera, performed in Toronto and Nova Scotia, was about an enslaved girl in Nova Scotia. Measha's performance was so captivating that in 2000 it was filmed for CBC-TV.

Measha's artistic reach spans far and wide. She has performed with orchestras around the world, including the Toronto Symphony Orchestra, the Montreal Symphony Orchestra, and the Thunder Bay Symphony Orchestra. She's performed in Carnegie Hall in New York and the Sydney Opera House in Australia. In 2007, she was a soloist at the Royal Nova Scotia International Tattoo. Measha has sung for Queen Elizabeth II in the United States, and at the Royal Albert Hall in London, England. She also had the honour of singing the "Olympic Hymn," in both French and English, to open the 2010 winter games in Vancouver, while 3.2 billion viewers watched from around the world.

Measha's talent has been recognized many times throughout her career. She has been nominated for two Juno Awards (Canada) and one Grammy (United States). In 2010, she won a Juno Award for Classical Album of the Year. Measha describes her talent as a gift from God and besides entertaining audiences and royalty in great halls and stadiums, she also uses her voice to help others. She is part of a Canadian charity called Artists Against Racism. In 2007, Measha travelled to Patongo in East Africa and sang to children as musical therapy.

DID YOU KNOW?

Measha is a descendant of former enslaved people John and Rose Gosman. The couple escaped slavery during the American Revolutionary War, and are recorded in the Book of Negroes *as passengers on one of the last ships to leave New York for Nova Scotia in 1783.*

GEORGE ELLIOTT CLARKE

hen George Elliott Clarke was eight years old, his mother took him to a library that had just opened in the North End of Halifax. That Saturday, George's mother signed him up for his very own library card. George was so excited to read the many books that overflowed the shelves. He read almost every book in the children's section, and he loved some so much that he read them twice. By the time he was ten years old, the librarian gave George special permission to check out books meant for older readers. George was mesmerized by the world of Shakespeare, and African American poets like Langston Hughes.

Growing up in Halifax, George's family home was filled with art, music, and lively discussions about social issues. George loved music and even tried playing the trombone, but he eventually gave it up and decided writing would be his connection to music. He began writing lyrics when he was thirteen years old and started devoting more and more time to his writing by the time he was fifteen. He wrote four songs a day, every day, for four years. To become a better songwriter, George decided to study poetry. But the more he studied poetry, and after having a poem published when he was nineteen years old, he knew he wanted to be a poet.

Even so, George's poetry made it into the music world and his words have impressed some pretty big names. In 2017, the band U2 contacted George to request the use of two of his poems. George's beautiful words scrolled across large screens during one of their world tours. In addition to poetry, George is also a published novelist. His books focus on the history of Black Canadian communities of Nova Scotia and New Brunswick, with George using the term "Africadian" to include all parts of his identity.

George has received the Order of Canada and the **Governor General Award** for poetry. He served as Canadian Parliamentary **Poet Laureate** from 2016 to 2017. George's late great-aunt is Portia White, who was a famous classical opera singer from Nova Scotia.

"LASSO THE WIND"
By George Elliott Clarke

Can you burn down the sun?
Can you darken the moon?
Can you drown a mountain?
Can you bid stars to swoon?

Can you lasso the wind?
Can you whip it a-gale?
Can you make oceans bend
To cradle each lost whale?

–from George's book of children's poetry,
Lasso the Wind: Aurelia's Verses and Other Poems

DID YOU KNOW?

The Order of Canada is the second highest honour for merit in Canada. It comes second only to membership in the Order of Merit, which is a personal gift of Canada's monarch. The honour recognizes Canadians who have made a major and positive impact on the country. It is presented to recipients by the Governor General of Canada.

EDWARD MITCHELL BANNISTER

Edward Mitchell Bannister was a painter born in 1828 in a small coastal village called St. Andrews in New Brunswick. Edward's mother, Hannah, encouraged Edward to draw, and he was known around the neighbourhood for drawing crayon portraits of family members and classmates. Edward's parents died when he was a young boy, and he went to live with a foster family before becoming a cook on a boat—a common job for young men from St. Andrews. Edward's favourite part about working on a boat was visiting the museums and libraries in the various cities where they travelled.

In 1848, when he was twenty years old, Edward moved to Boston, Massachusetts, and worked a variety of jobs while taking evening art classes in the hopes of perfecting his craft. One of those jobs was as a barber in a Boston salon owned by successful businesswoman, Christina Carteaux. Edward and Christina married in 1857, and the couple was very active in Boston's social and political scene.

Because he was Black, Edward was unable to find an established artist who would accept him as a student. But in 1854 he received his first commission, for an oil painting called *The Ship Outward Bound*. He painted it for a Black doctor named John V. DeGrasse. A local newspaper called *The Liberator* reported on Edward's painting, which was of a ship with large sails leaving the harbour. The next year, a Black abolitionist named William Copper Nell said Edward was a rising young artist in his book *The Colored Patriots of the American Revolution*. Edward was becoming an established painter in the Boston area. In 1858, Edward was able to list his occupation as "artist" in Boston's city directory.

Amazing Black Atlantic Canadians

Edward typically painted portraits, landscapes, and scenes from history. In the mid-1860s, Edward was finally able to receive some formal training to master his craft as a painter. He was the only Black artist in his drawing class. While he is remembered mostly as a landscape artist, Edward advertised himself as a portrait painter at the start of his career to try to get more work. In the Black community, men and women were always seeing images of Black people that mocked them and made them look inferior or ridiculous. Having someone paint a proper, respectable picture of them was important and appreciated. And so portraits were in high demand as part of a way to earn respect.

Edward's name and his work were popping up in a number of Boston art reviews, but one of those articles was not so kind. In 1867, Edward read an article in the *New York Herald* that stated he was not a talented artist. Determined to prove this writer wrong, the negative remarks only made Edward work harder. Two years later, in 1869, Edward moved to Providence, Rhode Island, and began to be recognized by the area's growing arts community. His first exhibit included a painting called *Newspaper Boy*, which was

Edward and his wife, Christina, advocated for human rights and social justice. The couple were part of a fundraiser to support Black soldiers who were being paid less than white soldiers in the union army. Christina also established a nursing home for elderly Black women.

one of the earliest portraits of a working-class Black boy painted by a Black artist. In 1876, Edward's painting *Under the Oaks*, which was inspired by a nearby farm, won the first-prize medal at the Philadelphia Centennial Exposition, making him the first Black artist to receive a national award.

Edward went on to exhibit his work all over the United States, including Boston, Providence, New York City, New Orleans, Detroit, and Hartford. His work was in demand by New England galleries and collectors. He also taught art classes and went on to receive several more awards and honours.

MAXINE TYNES

Maxine Tynes grew up in the 1950s in the heart of downtown Dartmouth, beside the railway. Maxine's childhood home was always filled with neighbourhood children, and her father would also bring people he met at work home with him for dinner. Maxine's father worked at the shipyard, which was just a five-minute walk from their home. People came into the shipyard from all over the world, and Maxine's father always took it upon himself to welcome them to his city.

Maxine's ancestors were Black Loyalists who migrated to Nova Scotia in the 1700s. When Maxine was four years old, she was diagnosed with polio, a disease that left her paralyzed from her right hip down to her right foot. When she became really ill, she had to stay home from school for a few years and her mother became her schoolteacher. Maxine's mother was always telling her children that they could do anything and be anything. Maxine often heard things like, "If something's worth doing, it's worth doing well," and "If you don't believe in yourself, nobody else will."

Once she was back at elementary school, Maxine began filling notebooks with stories. Her teacher was so impressed with her stories that she would take Maxine around to different classrooms and have her read her writing to some of the older students, which made Maxine nervous, but also very proud. Maxine discovered her love of writing poetry in high school. She wrote what she felt—what made her happy, what made her sad, and what angered her, like racism and war. Her first book of poetry was published in 1987. It was called *Borrowed Beauty* and it received the Milton Acorn People's Poetry Award, earning her the title of People's Poet of Canada.

Maxine also used her passion for the English language to teach. She aspired to be as wonderful a teacher as her mother was and she certainly succeeded. Maxine was a beloved high school English teacher and loved sharing a wide variety of poetry with her students. In 1993, she was awarded a Canadian medal from the Governor General. She passed away in 2011, and since then, the Alderney Gate Public Library in downtown Dartmouth has named one of their gathering rooms "The Maxine Tynes Room" to honour her memory.

"I'M A KID OF THE WORLD"
By Maxine Tynes

I am one of the kids of the
    world,
a kid of the world that's free.
I'm not too big or tall or small—
my part of the world just nicely
    fits me.

Sometimes I lie about in the sun
sometimes I hang out in trees
sometimes I'm just so full of
    beans
my energy zips me around like
    the breeze.

I'm one of the kids you might
    see on your block
on your street or down a dirt
    road.
When I'm alone I explore and
    I'm quiet
but when we're a bunch
we shout and we laugh like a
    riot.
I'm a kid of the world
    and I like it just fine.
If you take care of it now
    someday its care will be mine.

–From Maxine's book of poetry *Save the World For Me*,
published by Pottersfield Press in 1990

ALIYAH LAILSON

Aliyah Lailson wanted to become a published author before she was fourteen years old. Aliyah was born in 2005 in St. Catharines, Ontario, but now lives with her family in Halifax. In 2018, she found out about a writing contest hosted by Woozles Children's Bookstore in Halifax. At just thirteen years old, Aliyah, along with another young writer, found out her book, *North Wind*, had won the contest—the prize was publication! Aliyah's twin sister, Rebekah, was a finalist in the poetry competition. *North Wind* is about a boy who goes on a journey in a land full of magic. Since Aliyah's first book was published when she was just thirteen years old, that makes her the youngest published Black Canadian author.

PORTIA WHITE

Portia White was named after a Shakespeare character in a play called *The Merchant of Venice*. After the First World War, Portia's parents, William A. White and Izie Dora White, and her twelve brothers and sisters moved to Halifax from Truro. The Whites were a talented musical family, and Portia was no exception. Portia's father, William, was a pastor, and Portia began singing in the church's choir when she was six years old. Members of the church choir would come to the Whites' home after Sunday service and continue singing with the family. Portia's mother, Izie, was an accomplished singer who also played the mandolin and harpsichord. Izie gave her children piano and singing lessons.

When she grew up, Portia became a schoolteacher and she taught in a segregated school in Africville. Once school was out for the day, Portia would rush to voice lessons. She loved to sing and she practised every day. Portia walked sixteen kilometres a week to attend her music lessons. On November 7, 1941, Portia made her formal debut as a contralto at Toronto's Eaton Auditorium. She was thirty years old. She sang several different types of music in several different languages, including classical European music and Black spiritual music. Many described her voice as "a gift from heaven."

Portia performed in almost one hundred recitals in Canada, the United States, South America, and the Caribbean. She was asked to give a special performance for Queen Elizabeth II and Prince Philip at the opening of the Confederation Centre of Arts in Charlottetown, Prince Edward Island, in 1964. Portia's beautiful voice made her the first Black Canadian concert singer to be known around the world.

Amazing Black Atlantic Canadians

Portia became ill just a few years after reaching worldwide success and was unable to continue performing. But that didn't stop her from continuing to share her gift of music through teaching. Portia was in high demand to train aspiring theatre and television performers. In 1995, the Government of Canada named Portia a "person of national significance."

REMEMBERING PORTIA

Portia White has been honoured in many different ways. In 1999, she was featured in a special issue of millennium postage stamps celebrating Canadian achievement. A Halifax street was renamed Portia White Court, and the Portia White Atrium is located within the Spatz Theatre at Citadel High School in downtown Halifax. A local artist carved a life-sized sculpture of Portia from an elm tree in 2004. The sculpture is located in front of Zion Baptist Church in Truro, where Portia's father was the pastor.

DID YOU KNOW?

The very first Portia White prize was awarded in 1998 to Portia's great-nephew, poet and writer George Elliott Clarke.

SYLVIA HAMILTON

s a young girl, Sylvia Hamilton rarely saw on television or read books about people who looked like her. In high school, she went to her first non-segregated school and noticed all of the textbooks didn't really mention any Black history. From that moment, Sylvia knew she wanted to find out more about her ancestors and wanted to tell the stories that no one else was telling. And she's found many creative ways to tell those stories.

As a filmmaker, Sylvia goes behind the camera and captures others who share their triumphs and struggles as Black Canadians through her film company called Maroon Films. As a poet, she's written poems about hope, hurt, and faith. Sylvia gives a voice to Black men, women, and children who may otherwise not be heard.

Her documentary films have appeared in festivals around the world and have been broadcast on several television networks. Sylvia's first film, *Black Mother Black Daughter*, was made with an entirely female crew, making it the first film out of the Atlantic studio of the National Film Board to be run completely by women.

In 2000, Sylvia released a documentary about contralto opera singer Portia White called *Portia White: Think on Me*. Fittingly, in 2002, Sylvia received the Portia White Prize, which recognizes artistic excellence and achievement by a Nova Scotian artist.

When Sylvia began teaching at the School of Journalism at the University of King's College in Halifax, her goal was to open her students up to the world around them. Her hope is that they will have far more experiences than she did when she was that young girl attending an integrated high school and craving to learn more about her history and her ancestors.

SCOTT PARSONS

Scott Parsons is a storyteller. As a singer, songwriter, and guitarist, Scott finds melodic ways to tell the stories of other Black men and women in his hometown of Prince Edward Island. Scott's own story on the island began when he was a young boy in the sixties and his family moved from Halifax. Scott attended a one-room schoolhouse with nine grades all under one roof. When Scott was first perfecting his musical craft, he studied under some of the best on the Island. It wasn't long before he had created his own unique sound that was influenced by folk, blues, reggae, country, and rock music.

Scott works hard to incorporate local Black history into his music. Scott's first album—and one of his band names—was *Jupiter Wise*, which was the name of an enslaved person who had lived on Prince Edward Island. Scott read about Jupiter and realized he was living in the same neighbourhood where Jupiter had lived on the island, called the Bog. Scott's third album, *Darkie's Hollow*, was named after a local gathering place on Seven Mile Road where Black families would stop to enjoy an evening of music and socializing. "Hattie's Prayer" is about a well-known Islander, Hattie Hughes. Scott has also written a song about legendary Black boxer George Godfrey (see page 51), who was known as "Old Chocolate."

Scott loves sharing these stories of amazing Black Atlantic Canadians through song, and he's also teaching younger generations how to do the same. He's given free guitar lessons and taught drama to students in Charlottetown. Scott also used to perform a puppet show for local schools that taught kids about how people with different challenges and disabilities just want to be treated like everyone else.

In 1993, the United Nations used Scott's song "What I Am" as the theme song for the International Convention for the Rights of the Child in Victoria, British Columbia. From composing award-winning soundtracks for films to working in television and radio, Scott always finds ways to celebrate the tales of Black Islanders and share their incredible stories.

EDITH CLAYTON

As a young girl in Cherry Brook, Nova Scotia, in the 1900s, Edith Clayton would watch her mother craft beautiful wooden baskets. Edith made her first basket when she was just eight years old. Edith's technique to create her baskets originated in Africa and was passed down from mother to daughter over six generations. Edith got natural dyes from local Mi'kmaw women to colour the wood for her baskets.

For Edith and many basket weavers, the art of basket weaving was more than a hobby; it was a way to earn money to buy food and other household necessities. Historically, when Black families arrived in Nova Scotia after the War of 1812, they were given land with tough soil and had trouble harvesting any crops. Basket weavers would create items to sell at local markets to support their families.

Edith was a regular at the Halifax Farmers' Market for many years. Her baskets were so unique and beautiful that Edith was asked to represent Canada at Expo '86 in Vancouver, British Columbia. It was certainly an honour to be part of such a large event, which featured exhibitions from all over the world. The theme of the world fair was "World in Motion—World in Touch," and more than 22 million people were dazzled by gondolas, movie theatres, restaurants, shops, singing, dancing, and so much more.

Edith's baskets can be found in homes and exhibits around the world. Edith's daughters have now proudly continued the tradition of basket making, passed down from their mother as it has been for generations. These women are able to pull strips of raw red maple wood together to form a beautiful basket in just a few hours.

While techniques and styles have changed throughout the years, the love and care put into each basket is just as strong as when Edith was a little girl learning how to weave her first basket.

CHARLES "BUCKY" ADAMS

Charles "Bucky" Adams was part of a large musical family that lived in Halifax. He began playing musical instruments when he was six years old, starting with the trumpet to accompany his father, who played the saxophone. When he was eight years old, he got a job playing the trumpet for the Barnum & Bailey Circus during their visit in Halifax. Members of the band heard Bucky playing on his front doorstep as they were walking by and asked him to join them on the Halifax Commons. Bucky loved music and he taught himself how to play several musical instruments, including the bugle, the trumpet, and the tenor sax. He played all sorts of different styles of music, from swing and R&B, to jazz, and blues. It wasn't long before people were starting to take notice of Bucky's incredible musical abilities. At age eleven, Bucky played trumpet for the Queen of England during one of her royal visits to Halifax. Bucky has played with, or performed for, jazz greats like Louis Armstrong, Dizzie Gillespie, Oscar Peterson, and B. B. King. In 1998, Bucky was even asked to perform for American civil rights pioneer, Rosa Parks.

THE SHOW MUST GO ON!

During one of Bucky's performances at the Gerrish Street Hall in Halifax, he played his trumpet with so much intensity that it literally blew apart. In between sets, he ran home and borrowed his father's tenor saxophone, returning just in time to get back on stage and continue the show. Ever since that show, Bucky loved playing the tenor sax.

Amazing Black Atlantic Canadians

PART IV

MOVERS AND SHAKERS

"The winds of change are blowing throughout Nova Scotia.... We can do the job provided that we are given the opportunity and provided that we are treated as equals."

–Calvin Ruck, social worker, human rights activist, senator

"We try to make sure that as many people know about [Sharing Our Cultures] as possible so that they can come and learn and through that process of learning they can find somewhere in their heart to accept diversity and to respect people who are not like them. We all have the same heart that's beating within us."

–Lloydetta Quaicoe, community activist

MOVERS AND SHAKERS

t's amazing what one person can do. One person can refuse to sit in the balcony at a movie theatre and change the course of history forever. One person can fight for basic human rights like a haircut and ensure no one is ever denied that right again. One person can take a stand against violence in their hometown and end up inspiring people around the world. The following movers and shakers didn't decide to take a stand for fame and glory. These men and women have shown courage and strength and they have made a difference just by doing what was right. And they've worked hard to achieve great things. They've gone the extra mile to learn more, study harder, and even started brand new careers in the hopes of helping others. They've shown us that knowledge is power and education really can help you achieve great things. And that's pretty amazing.

VIOLA DESMOND

ost people know Viola Desmond as the first Black woman to appear on the Canadian ten-dollar bill. But before she was known for taking a stand against Nova Scotia's racist laws in 1946, she was also a savvy businesswoman and successful entrepreneur. Viola travelled to Montreal to study to become a beautician, and when she returned to Halifax a year later, she opened Vi's Studio of Beauty Culture. But her desire to share her knowledge and skill didn't stop there. She wanted to help other Black women achieve their goals in the beauty industry. She also wanted to create beauty products tailored to Black women and their specific beauty needs. She began concocting face powders, creating pomades for Black hair, and designing fashionable wigs. In 1944, Viola opened the Desmond School of Beauty Culture in Halifax. It was the very first school in all of Canada to train Black beauty culturists.

Viola never set out to be a public figure for the fight against racism, but on November 8, 1946, in New Glasgow, Nova Scotia, Viola decided she had had enough, and took a stand. She was tired after a long day of driving on a sales trip for her beauty products. When she arrived in New Glasgow, her car began making strange noises. She decided to take it to a local mechanic who told her it would not be fixed until the next morning. With nothing to do for the evening, Viola decided to see a movie at the Roseland Theatre.

Unbeknownst to Viola, the theatre had a policy that Black moviegoers only sat in the balcony and were not allowed to sit downstairs with the white patrons. Viola was also unaware that despite asking to purchase a ticket for downstairs, she was given a balcony ticket because she was Black. When Viola took her seat downstairs, she was promptly asked to move. But she was tired and determined to sit where she wanted. Soon, a police officer arrived and Viola was dragged out of the theatre and into the street. She was taken to jail and the next day Viola was charged with not paying the full price for a downstairs seat, which was a single penny more than a balcony seat. Viola explained that she had tried to pay for the downstairs ticket, but she was denied the right because of the colour of her skin. She paid a fine and returned home immediately.

Viola knew what happened to her wasn't right, and when she returned home, her family and friends encouraged her to appeal her conviction. Viola's case went all the way to the Supreme Court of Nova Scotia. She may have lost her appeal, but Black Atlantic Canadians were inspired by her bravery, and now motivated to speak up for their rights and fight discrimination.

Viola took a stand that day and her brave act has inspired countless others to do the same. It wouldn't be until several decades later that her courage would be honoured.

HONOURING VIOLA: A TIMELINE

◊ On April 15, 2010, Viola Desmond received the first **posthumous pardon** in Canada, granted by the first Black lieutenant-governor of Nova Scotia, the Honorable Mayann Francis (see page 133).

◊ On July 7, 2016, Halifax Transit launched their newest ferry, named the *Viola Desmond*.

◊ In 2017, Viola was inducted into Canada's Walk of Fame on Simcoe Street in Toronto.

◊ In 2018, the Government of Canada named Viola a Person of National Historic Significance. That same year, she became the first woman, besides the Queen of England, to be featured on a Canadian bank note. The purple ten-dollar bill features Viola's portrait and a vertical map of North End Halifax, where Viola lived and worked, along with an excerpt from the **Canadian Charter of Rights and Freedoms**. The Canadian Museum of Human Rights is pictured on the back of the bill.

DID YOU KNOW?

Viola's family lived in North End Halifax on Gottingen Street. On the morning of December 6, 1917, three-year-old Viola was sitting in her high chair eating breakfast when a thunderous noise shook the house and shattered the kitchen window behind her. A window blind fell on top of Viola, but she was not injured. The Desmond family would soon find out the damage was caused by the Halifax Explosion, which killed approximately 2,000 people and injured 9,000 more.

WANDA ROBSON

anda Robson is Viola Desmond's youngest sister. Wanda used to help Viola with her beauty supply business, mixing creams and packaging products for Viola's customers, but Wanda always dreamt of earning a university degree. So in 2000, when Wanda was in her seventies, she enrolled at Cape Breton University. One of Wanda's courses was about race relations. While sitting in class one day, the professor, Graham Reynolds, began talking about Viola Desmond and her fight against racism and discrimination. Wanda raised her hand and said, "That's my sister!" It was in that class that Wanda realized the true significance of her sister's arrest and the injustice that had been done all those years ago.

Wanda was determined to do everything she could to acknowledge her sister and right the wrongs of the past. In 2004, at seventy-six years of age, Wanda graduated with a Bachelor of Arts degree from Cape Breton University. She's written books about Viola's life and courage, and she's spoken across the country. Her efforts have resulted in Canadians discovering all kinds of ways to honour a Canadian hero, including a postage stamp and the ten-dollar bill. Wanda has worked hard to make sure people know her sister's legacy.

ZAINAB JERRETT

The sweet and savoury smells of perfect spice blends drew large crowds to Zainab Jerrett's Multi Ethnic Food Kitchen at the St. John's Farmers' Market for more than a decade. In 2019, after eleven years as part of the market's "heart and soul," she retired. It all began when Zainab first went to the market with a friend many years ago, and brought just two African dishes to share with customers. She was fairly new to the culinary scene. In fact, Zainab didn't cook at all until she travelled from Nigeria to Newfoundland in 1992 to complete her Ph.D. in folklore at Memorial University. Her roommates came from all over the world and Zainab loved all of the different dishes they would prepare. She wanted to learn how to make them and that's how her love for cooking and feeding others began.

Market-goers were immediately drawn to Zainab's bright smile, but they kept coming back for her delicious food. From samosas and beef patties to butter chicken and yellow rice, Zainab loves introducing people to new cultures, new experiences, and new food. It wasn't long after her arrival in Newfoundland that she became an integral part of the St. John's community. But for Zainab it's about far more than filling plates with delicious offerings. After catering the Tombolo Multicultural Festival, which promotes cultural diversity and helps newcomers immigrate into the province, Zainab discovered the organizers were getting ready to shut the festival down. She didn't want the multicultural events to end, so she decided to take on the role of executive director to keep it going. And, like the name Tombolo, which means a piece of land that connects, the events bring diverse cultures together through concerts, workshops, and of course, food. Newfoundland's ever-popular International Food and Craft Fair also came under Zainab's direction when it became too big to manage and was going to end.

Zainab began selling crafts in Newfoundland that were created by women in rural parts of Africa, including Nigeria, Kenya, Chad, and Niger. Colourful jewellery, bright fabrics, and Zainab's popular food were all it took for her to become a success. But a piece of her heart will always be in Nigeria, and that is why she started the We Care Foundation of Newfoundland and Labrador. The foundation supports women and youth in northeastern Nigeria who were affected by military violence. Zainab wants to help them integrate back into society and get the girls back into schools. In 2018, the foundation filled six cars and one school bus with clothing, books, and school supplies. The vehicles were shipped to Nigeria and the boxes were handed out to those in need. The bus was then used for the children to get to and from school safely.

When Zainab first arrived in Newfoundland, she had always planned on returning to Nigeria after she completed her university degree, but she ended up finding a purpose and place in the Atlantic province and continues to find new and inventive ways to bring people together, to celebrate diversity, and to give back.

CALVIN RUCK

n 1945, when Calvin Ruck was twenty years old, he worked as a sleeping-car porter with the Canadian National Railway, attending to the passengers' needs during their journeys. He carried luggage, made beds, shined shoes, and served food and drinks. When Calvin started having a family of his own, he wanted to stay closer to his home in Halifax.

When he found out certain Black communities didn't have access to basic services like running water and paved roads, he knew he wanted to help. He started a small dry-cleaning business, sold school supplies and candy, and worked with others in the community to build a baseball field, medical clinic, and daycare. These community interests led Calvin to become a social worker and social activist who worked tirelessly to ensure Black men and women were provided jobs, paved roads, and running water.

When his oldest son, Douglas, told Calvin he had been denied a haircut at a local barbershop, Calvin immediately returned to the shop with his youngest son, Martin, and insisted the barber cut his hair. When the barber again refused, Calvin lobbied the community, contacted the media and the human rights commission, and ensured that barber, and many others in the city, would no longer be able to refuse haircuts based on the colour of a client's skin.

Calvin also had to fight to be able to build his family home on an empty plot in Dartmouth. When the residents found out a Black man was moving into their mostly white neighbourhood, they gathered together and signed a petition to try to stop him. Despite their racist efforts, Calvin was able to prove he was capable of building a home that was just as good as everyone else's. And his family lived in that neighbourhood for almost fifty years.

In 1998, Calvin became the third Black Canadian appointed to the Senate of Canada. He received several honours during his lifetime, including the Order of Canada and honourary degrees from Dalhousie University and the University of King's College.

DID YOU KNOW?

Men and women across Canada are asked to become senators by the prime minister of Canada. Senators have meetings in the Senate Chamber and discuss all kinds of different topics that affect Canadians. An idea for a new law is called a bill, and both the Senate and the House of Commons have to approve the bill before it becomes law.

Amazing Black Atlantic Canadians

DOUGLAS RUCK

Growing up, Douglas Ruck was one of only a few Black children in his school. Douglas's father, Calvin, taught him how to box at a young age so he was always ready to properly defend himself against bullies who picked on him because of the colour of his skin.

Like his father, Douglas knew he wanted to help people. He went to the University of King's College in Halifax and was voted **valedictorian** of his graduating class in 1972. He went on to study law at Dalhousie University and opened his own law firm in Halifax. In 1995, Douglas became the first Black **ombudsman** of Nova Scotia. Douglas was instrumental in the creation of the Children's Ombudsman for Nova Scotia, a role that ensures all children in the province have a voice. In 2011, Douglas was named the first chair of the Nova Scotia labour board.

BURNLEY ALLAN "ROCKY" JONES AND JOAN JONES

urnley Allan Jones was born in a small Black community called the Marsh on the outskirts of Truro, Nova Scotia. "Rocky" was a nickname he gave himself after he joined the army when he was just sixteen years old. Three years later, in 1959, Rocky took a job driving a tractor-trailer truck in Toronto. That's when he met his first wife, Joan. Joan was the one who introduced Rocky to the civil rights movement. Rocky began reading books and attending talks in Toronto about social justice and human rights. It wasn't long before Rocky became an outspoken activist.

In 1965, Rocky and Joan left Ontario to live in Halifax. Rocky, Joan, and other members of their community would gather at their kitchen table and discuss what they could do to make a difference. When the kitchen table could no longer hold all of the people who wanted to help, the couple opened up Kwacha House on Gottingen Street in 1967, eastern Canada's first inner-city self-help program. Kwacha House was a place to talk, to share ideas, and for Black and white youth to come together and try to work out their differences.

In the early sixties, Rocky and Joan became friends with social activist and well-known Black Panther Stokely Carmichael, and Stokely's wife, Mariam. The Black Panthers were an African American group that fought for Black rights in the United States.

When the American couple travelled to Halifax to visit the Jones family and stayed in their home, Rocky and Joan became immediate targets of police surveillance. Their phones were tapped, police sat outside their home and watched their comings and goings, and the media began calling Rocky "Rocky the Revolutionary." Rocky had no intention of encouraging violence, but because he fought for equality, he became a target. Rocky knew his family was being watched, and sometimes he would approach the unmarked vehicles parked outside his home and offer the officers coffee in the morning. He even jokingly asked them for a ride since he knew they would be going wherever he was going. Stokely and Mariam returned to the United States, but the police never really left Rocky alone.

It also became difficult for Rocky to find a job. No one wanted to hire someone who they thought would cause trouble. He and Joan eventually started their own business, specializing in leatherwork. Their resourcefulness kept food on their table and their five children clothed. They continued to open up their home to anyone who needed a safe place, including many foster children.

Among other organizations, Rocky co-founded the Black United Front of Nova Scotia and the National Black Coalition of Canada. Both organizations were all about empowering Black communities to stand up for their rights. The Black United Front formed its own police force to try to keep hard drugs out of Halifax communities and they built a park for young children called the Tot-Lot. Rocky and its members found ways to improve the lives of Black people in the province through better jobs, better homes, and better education.

DID YOU KNOW?

The majority of sleeping-car porters were Black men. Porters were known as geographical experts. They rode the rails every single day and knew more about Canada and its landmarks than most Canadians.

A HOME AWAY FROM HOME

ocky and Joan Jones lived in a large house on Windsor Street in Halifax and they had many amazing Black Nova Scotian friends who would frequently stop by for a visit. When he was younger, poet and author George Elliott Clarke (see page 70) would visit the Jones family as much as he could. He would knock on the door, be given a plate of food, and then head straight for the one room in the home that was designated as a library. George loved spending time in that room reading books and listening to the family's large record collection with music mostly from the sixties. George also enjoyed talking to actor and writer Walter Borden (see page 65) while visiting the Jones family library. Walter lived with the Jones family for a little while as they worked on creating Kwacha House and other human rights initiatives.

CARRIE BEST

Just like Viola Desmond, Carrie Mae Best and her son, Calbert, were arrested at the Roseland Theatre in New Glasgow after sitting in the downstairs "whites-only" section of the theatre.

In 1941, five years before Viola would visit the theatre, Carrie heard that several Black teenage girls had been kicked out of the theatre after trying to sit in the section on the main level. After speaking with the theatre's owner, who ignored Carrie's protest of the racist policy, Carrie and her fifteen-year-old son decided to go to the theatre themselves. The cashier insisted they take tickets for the balcony, but Carrie refused. She and Calbert walked into the main level of the theatre and took their seats. When police arrived, they were forcefully removed and charged with disturbing the peace.

Carrie filed a **civil lawsuit** against the theatre for racial discrimination, but the judge decided the theatre's owner had a right to deny service. Frustrated, Carrie wanted to find a way to fight back against racism, and if the courts weren't going to listen to her, she would have to find another way to have her voice heard.

Carrie and Calbert started a newspaper called *The Clarion* in 1946—one of the first newspapers in Nova Scotia owned and operated by Black Canadians. *The Clarion* reported on sports, news, and social activities. Carrie used *The Clarion* to advocate for social justice, including sharing all of the details of Viola Desmond's trial, and publicly showing her firm support of Viola.

Besides publishing the newspaper, Carrie also started a radio show called *The Quiet Corner* in 1952. Carrie played classical and religious music and read poetry in between songs. The show remained on the air for twelve years, and was broadcasted on four radio stations in the Maritimes. Carrie has been honoured several times for her work as a journalist and social activist. She's been awarded the Queen Elizabeth Medal, the Order of Nova Scotia, and the Order of Canada. Carrie was inducted into the Nova Scotia Black Wall of Fame, and a postage stamp to honour her work was released February 1, 2011.

DID YOU KNOW?

The first Nova Scotia newspaper owned and operated by Black Canadians was called The Atlantic Advocate. *The newspaper was first published in 1915 by Miriam A. DeCosta, Wilfred A. DeCosta, who was a member of the No. 2 Construction Battalion, and Dr. Clement Courtenay Ligoure, who opened a private medical practice in his house in Halifax's North End where he treated victims of the 1917 Halifax Explosion. The Atlantic Advocate was a monthly journal that covered several topics about, and that would be of interest to, Black Atlantic Canadians. Articles included stories about Black men and women making a difference, the importance of family, and racism in Atlantic Canada. The newspaper had a short run in circulation and shut down in 1917.*

REVEREND WILLIAM PEARLY OLIVER

illiam Pearly Oliver loved playing sports while growing up in Wolfville, Nova Scotia. And he proved to be a pretty good athlete and a pretty good leader, too. In his senior year at Wolfville High School, William was captain of both the football and hockey teams, and was an impressive long-distance runner.

He enrolled at Acadia University in 1930. William played water polo and hockey, and was on the relay team for track and field. In 1934, he graduated with a Bachelor of Arts. He then returned to Acadia and in 1936 he graduated with a bachelor of divinity, which focuses on theology and religion. He was the first Black Nova Scotian to obtain two university degrees.

The next year, in 1937, William became the pastor of Halifax's Cornwallis Street Baptist Church, making him the church's

DID YOU KNOW?

Viola Desmond and her husband, Jack, attended Cornwallis Street Baptist Church, where Reverend Oliver was the pastor. The morning after Viola's arrest in New Glasgow, she went to the Olivers' home to seek advice and support. William's wife, Pearleen, was so upset about what had happened. She told Viola to receive immediate medical attention for her injuries, and encouraged her to take her case to court.

youngest pastor ever. This church is now known as New Horizons Baptist Church and is called the "mother church" because it was the first church in the province owned and operated by Black people. William stayed there for twenty-five years. The only pastor to serve longer was the church's founder, Richard Preston.

In 1942, William joined the army and served as the only Black Canadian army chaplain during the Second World War. He worked with recruits in Halifax and he was only allowed to minister to the Black troops.

In 1962, William left his position at the church to begin a new career as an adult educator. Starting a new career at fifty years old was scary, but William was looking forward to taking on something new. He believed education was important to succeed in life, and he wanted to do what he could to give Black students a chance to succeed. Black students weren't given the same opportunities as others because of the colour of their skin. They weren't allowed to go to certain schools, they were often denied a higher education, and many had to drop out of school when they were young to work and support their family. That's why William established scholarships for Black students seeking higher education.

In 1983, William founded the Black Cultural Centre of Nova Scotia. He also played a key role in forming the Nova Scotia Association for the Advancement of Coloured People in 1945, the Nova Scotia Human Rights Commission in 1967, and the Black United Front in 1969. In 1985, William was invested into the Order of Canada.

The Nova Scotia Association for the Advancement of Coloured People was formed in 1945 with the goal of improving the standard of living for Black Nova Scotians. In 1947, the association took the case of Viola Desmond to the Supreme Court of Canada. The request to the court to have Viola's conviction thrown out was dismissed, because Viola's lawyer did not file the proper papers on time. The association also worked with the provincial board of education to ensure Victoria Cross recipient William Edward Hall be included in school history books.

NOVA SCOTIA HUMAN RIGHTS COMMISSION

The Nova Scotia Human Rights Commission was established in 1967. The commission addresses issues of discrimination and works towards equality and social justice.

GORDON EARLE

Gordon Earle's father worked as a sleeping-car porter on the railway. Gordon was the first employee of the Nova Scotia Human Rights Commission. In 1982, Gordon became the first Black ombudsman of Manitoba. Gordon was elected the first Black Member of Parliament from Nova Scotia in 1997 and represented the riding of Halifax West from 1997 to 2000. But politics isn't the only area where Gordon has achieved great success. He is also a martial artist with a black belt in karate. Gordon founded The Hammonds Plains Karate Club, where other budding martial artists could hone their craft.

BLACK CULTURAL CENTRE OF NOVA SCOTIA

The Black Cultural Centre of Nova Scotia opened its doors in 1983 in Cherry Brook, Nova Scotia. The centre is a museum and library, which holds the history of Black Nova Scotians. Inside, visitors can explore a bookstore, exhibition rooms, and an auditorium for special events.

H. A. J. (GUS) WEDDERBURN

Gus Wedderburn was born in Jamaica and came to Nova Scotia in 1957. Gus worked as a principal and started a tutoring program in East Preston that helped many students reach their goal of graduating from high school. In 1970, when he was forty-one years old, Gus switched careers and went to law school in Halifax. As a lawyer, Gus continued to mentor young people and assist disadvantaged communities. Gus was one of the founders of the Black Educator's Association, the Black United Front, the Nova Scotia Human Rights Commission, and the Black Cultural Centre. He was also president of the Nova Scotia Association for the Advancement of Coloured People.

DR. ALTHEA PEARLEEN (BORDEN) OLIVER

Dr. Pearleen Oliver was born into a family of ten children in Cooks Cove, Guysborough County, Nova Scotia. Pearleen became the first Black graduate of New Glasgow High School in 1936. After graduation, Pearleen married Reverend William Pearly Oliver. Together with her husband, Pearleen was a founding member of the Black Cultural Centre, the Nova Scotia Association for the Advancement of Colored People, the Nova Scotia Human Rights Commission, and the Black United Front. As a young girl, Pearleen had dreamt of becoming a nurse, but when she tried to apply to nursing school, she was rejected because she was Black. Pearleen, along with the Nova Scotia Association for the Advancement of Colored People, fought to have the Children's Hospital of Halifax allow Black women to attend its nursing school. Pearleen also fought to ensure Black men and women were not only treated fairly, but also represented properly in school textbooks.

DR. BOLUWAJI OGUNYEMI

oluwaji Ogunyemi was eleven years old when his parents packed up their belongings in Nigeria and brought him and his brother to Newfoundland in 1998. His mother and father wanted to give their children the best opportunities in life, and they decided Canada was the place to be. Boluwaji learned the importance of hard work, dedication, and sacrifice from his parents.

With the goal to become a doctor, Boluwaji knew he had many years of schooling ahead of him. He began his studies at Western University in London, Ontario. After completing a double major in sociology and medical science, he returned home to St. John's, Newfoundland and Labrador, and enrolled in medical school at Memorial University. Finally, he travelled to the University of British Columbia and was named the chief resident in the department of dermatology and skin science, and focused on refugee medicine.

WHAT IS REFUGEE MEDICINE?

Refugee medicine studies how the health of refugees is affected when they are forced to flee their homes. Refugees typically have to leave their home country and travel to another part of the world because of unsafe circumstances, such as war.

After completing his studies, Boluwaji returned to St. John's to work as a dermatologist, helping patients of all ages with skin diseases and severe drug reactions. Boluwaji's medical background has allowed him to travel around the world, including Lagos, Nigeria; Ho Chi Minh City, Vietnam; and Inuit communities in rural Labrador.

Boluwaji also writes about medicine, and has been published in the *New York Times*, *Huffington Post*, *Globe and Mail*, and *Vancouver Sun*. He's received multiple awards to celebrate his leadership, academic achievements, clinical research, and writing.

Boluwaji gives back to younger generations and is a mentor for youth in his community. Just like that eleven-year-old boy whose parents told him to dream big, Boluwaji wants to encourage youth from underrepresented backgrounds to pursue careers in health sciences.

LLOYDETTA QUAICOE

Newfoundlander Lloydetta Quaicoe wanted to create a high school program that would bring people of different cultures together, educate people on the diversity that exists in their own communities, and provide students with a space to share and celebrate their heritage. The idea came after she conducted a study on the needs of immigrant and refugee schoolchildren in Newfoundland and Labrador. Many students shared experiences of racism and discrimination, and Lloydetta wanted to help. Sharing Our Cultures was born.

The first showcase of Sharing Our Cultures was in 1999. Students set up informative displays, sang songs, performed traditional dances, and found many other creative ways to talk about their backgrounds and heritage. Over the past two decades, thousands of students and teachers have attended the annual event at schools in Labrador City, Happy Valley-Goose Bay, Corner Brook, Grand Falls, and Windsor.

Lloydetta also designs and publishes *Cultural Con'txt'*—a collection of poems, short stories, and drawings submitted by both French- and English-speaking students. For her countless hours of service to others and for making her community a better place, Lloydetta was honoured with the Queen Elizabeth II Diamond Jubilee Medal in 2013. In 2018, she was awarded the Human Rights Champion certificate from the Human Rights Commission of Newfoundland and Labrador.

QUENTREL PROVO

Quentrel Provo wanted to see change in his Halifax community. He was tired of hearing about Black people losing their lives or being treated unfairly because of the colour of their skin, and he knew something needed to be done. When he lost his cousin to gun violence in 2012, he decided to stop talking and start doing. When he was twenty-five years old, Quentrel started a movement called Stop the Violence, Spread the Love. The organization is all about encouraging people to walk in love instead of hate. A month after losing his cousin, Quentrel organized his first peace march through the streets of Dartmouth and Halifax. Despite it being an extremely wet and windy September day, about three hundred people joined Quentrel to walk from Sullivan's Pond in Dartmouth and across the Macdonald Bridge to the Halifax Commons. Quentrel was touched and inspired to see so many people, who, like him, wanted to see a change in their city and to promote peace instead of violence. The province of Nova Scotia declared June 10 Stop the Violence Day.

Quentrel has a special place in his heart for young people and wants the next generation to have plenty of Black men and women they can look up to. When the movie *Black Panther* was released in 2018, the film featured the first Black superhero and a mostly Black cast. Quentrel wanted as many kids as possible to see this historic movie, so he decided to start a fundraiser. In just one day he raised over three thousand dollars, giving two hundred local kids the chance to see the film in theatres. But he didn't stop there. He continued to fundraise and was able to send another two hundred kids to see *Black Panther*.

In 2019, Quentrel was anonymously nominated for the United Nations 2019 Most Influential People of African Descent. The list also includes people like hockey superstar P. K. Subban and football star and activist Colin Kaepernick. This global organization recognized by the United Nations clearly thinks Quentrel is pretty amazing too.

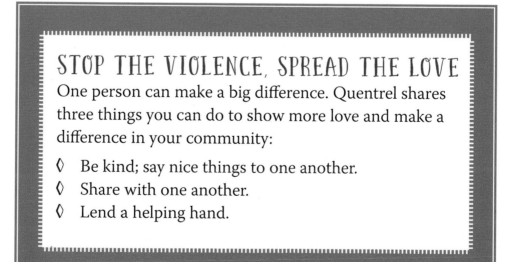

STOP THE VIOLENCE, SPREAD THE LOVE

One person can make a big difference. Quentrel shares three things you can do to show more love and make a difference in your community:

◊   Be kind; say nice things to one another.
◊   Share with one another.
◊   Lend a helping hand.

LENA O'REE

When Lena O'Ree put her mind to something, she was determined to get it done. In 1931, at seventeen years old, Lena hosted the first Black radio show in Saint John, New Brunswick. To ensure people would tune in, the radio station did not tell listeners they were listening to a Black woman.

In 1936, Lena went to the YWCA in hopes of joining the association. She was told if she wanted to join then she would have to get five other Black women to join with her. The next day, Lena returned to the YWCA with ten Black women ready to sign up.

In the 1950s, Lena worked as a housekeeper at a popular hotel in Saint John's called the Admiral Beatty. Black people were not allowed to go through the front door of the hotel. All guests, including Black celebrities like Louis Armstrong and Ella Fitzgerald, had to use the back door. Once Lena learned of this rule, she refused to show up for her shift until she was allowed to go through the front door. Lena's protest made national headlines and eventually the rule was changed and the colour barrier was removed from the Canadian Pacific Hotels chain across the country. Thanks to Lena, Black guests were also allowed to sit in the hotel dining rooms.

DR. CONSTANCE TIMBERLAKE

Constance Timberlake left her job working at a paintbrush manufacturer in New Brunswick to enrol in university in the United States to become a teacher. She eventually became a professor at Syracuse University in New York and an active member of the civil rights movement.

In 1963, Constance led a demonstration of sixteen Black and white protestors who entered Fairyland Park in Kansas City, bought tickets for the rides, and then lay on the ground to protest racial equality. Black people were not usually allowed at the park. Seven police cars arrived and the men and women were arrested and taken to jail for "disturbing the peace." The protestors sang **freedom songs** while being arrested. Constance continued to fight for human rights and was determined to have her voice heard.

PART V

MILITARY HEROES

" *We go on and on about our differences. But, you know, our differences are less important than our similarities. People have a lot in common with one another, whether they see that or not.* "

–William Hall

" *You couldn't get a job in a store or anywhere if you were Black, so we joined the Reserves.* "

–Corporal (Retired) Marelene Clyke

PART 5

MILITARY HEROES

lack men and women in Atlantic Canada have a long history of serving their country, but they weren't always welcome as Canadian soldiers. Many were told they were not fit to fight because of the colour of their skin. However, they pushed back against racism and discrimination to join the ranks as Canadian soldiers, and eventually travelled overseas to represent their country. These brave men and women put their lives at risk and many rose up to become national heroes.

Their acts of bravery were not always recognized, and for some, it would take many years before they received the recognition they deserved, including the highest and most prestigious awards given for bravery. They were proud Canadian soldiers and are an important part of Canadian history.

THE NO. 2 CONSTRUCTION BATTALION

When the First World War erupted in 1914, Canadians flocked to recruiting stations to fight for their country. Hundreds of Black Canadians were eager and ready to serve. But they were turned away. Black men were told it was a "white man's war" and were refused the right to fight. Some men were not ready to accept this and they began to protest. They sent letters to military officials and the government. They gained support from community members, both Black and white, and people began pressuring those in charge to change the rules and allow Black men to fight. By 1916, more and more men were dying overseas and able-bodied soldiers were desperately needed. Two years after the war had begun, the No. 2 Construction Battalion was officially authorized July 5, 1916, after the British War Office called the governor general and said they would accept an all-Black unit.

The battalion recruited across Canada. Nova Scotia had the most recruits with three hundred men. Their training headquarters were first in Pictou and then moved to Truro. The "Black Battalion" travelled aboard the SS *Southland* from Pier 2 in Halifax on March 28, 1917. Ten days later, they arrived in Liverpool, England.

Members of the Black Battalion weren't given the same necessary supplies given to other soldiers, and medical aid wasn't always available to Black soldiers. By May 1917, the battalion had lost a number of men who had become ill or died. The smaller unit, now called a company, was sent to the France and Switzerland border and joined the Canadian Forestry Corps, CEF, to perform logging duties. Logging was a dangerous and important task during wartime. Soldiers would have to cut down large trees in the forest and haul their heavy loads to a wood mill. The mill would turn the wood into whatever was needed to continue the war efforts, like railroad ties, shelters, and even explosives.

A GREAT LEGACY: A TIMELINE

The No. 2 Construction Battalion was officially disbanded September 15, 1920. The men of the No. 2 had fought racism and discrimination, but were still willing to risk their lives to serve their country. It would take decades before they were properly honoured as Canadian heroes. These are just some of the advancements achieved over the years.

November 2, 1982: Senator Calvin Ruck and the Black Cultural Society of Nova Scotia host a recognition and reunion banquet held at the Lord Nelson Hotel in Halifax for nine Black veterans who served in the First World War.

1986: Calvin Ruck writes *The Black Battalion 1916–1920: Canada's Best-Kept Military Secret*. The book shares the story of the No. 2 Construction Battalion and features pictures and personal stories from members of the battalion.

July 1993: Since the headquarters for the Black Battalion was first based at the Market Wharf in Pictou, Nova Scotia, a permanent monument is erected at Market Wharf to honour the No. 2 Construction Battalion in the summer of 1993. Hundreds gather there to honour and celebrate the battalion. The gathering has since become an annual celebration.

1997–1999: Calvin Ruck works with the department of Veterans Affairs to ensure each soldier of the Black Battalion receives a proper headstone and inscription. Before this, a simple flat white stone that was difficult to find marked each grave.

2001: Actor, director, writer, and producer Anthony Sherwood releases *Honour Before Glory*, a film based on the diary of the Black Battalion's chaplain, Reverend William A. White. Anthony is Reverend White's great-nephew and played the role of Reverend White in the film. In 2002, it won second prize at the Hollywood Black Film Festival in Los Angeles and won a Gemini Award. Anthony has worked on several films and plays about Black Canadian history, including a play about war hero William Hall in 2010.

February 1, 2016: An official commemorative stamp is launched by Canada Post to mark the 100th anniversary of the Black Battalion.

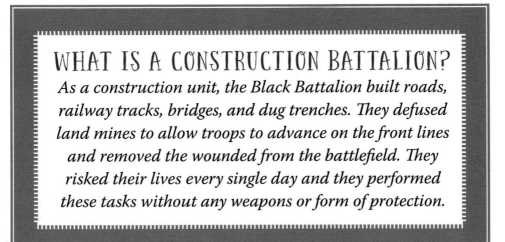

WHAT IS A CONSTRUCTION BATTALION?

As a construction unit, the Black Battalion built roads, railway tracks, bridges, and dug trenches. They defused land mines to allow troops to advance on the front lines and removed the wounded from the battlefield. They risked their lives every single day and they performed these tasks without any weapons or form of protection.

106TH BATTALION, NOVA SCOTIA RIFLES, CEF

The 106th Battalion was authorized November 8, 1915, during the First World War. Sixteen Black volunteers were accepted into the 106th Battalion. They hailed from Nova Scotia, Prince Edward Island, New Brunswick, and Newfoundland. When others got word of Black men being recruited for the war, protests erupted. On July 15, 1916, the battalion left for England aboard the RMS *Empress of Britain*. The soldiers provided reinforcements for frontline battalions who had lost several men in France.

REVEREND WILLIAM A. WHITE

evered William A. White was born in Virginia in 1874 and travelled to Canada in 1900 to study religion at Acadia University in Wolfville, Nova Scotia. William graduated in 1903, becoming only the second Black person to graduate from Acadia.

After graduation, he worked as a missionary and travelled to Black communities and churches across Nova Scotia before being named chaplain of the No. 2 Construction Battalion. This made him the first Black officer in the British Army. He took great care of his soldiers and was always concerned they weren't getting the same supplies as their fellow white soldiers.

In the early 1930s, William started a series of popular monthly radio broadcasts of his church services. People across Canada and in the northern United States could tune in and listen to his preaching. During the Great Depression, William set up a program to raise $2,500 a year to create trade schools in Black churches.

In 1936, William became the first Black Canadian to receive an honorary doctorate from Acadia University.

DID YOU KNOW?

Members of the White family were very well-known, not only in their community, but across Canada. William and his wife, Izie, had thirteen children, including Portia White (see page 78). Another of William and Izie's sons, Bill, was a composer and social activist who went on to become the first Black Canadian to run for federal office in 1949. Jack White was a well-known politician and Canadian labour union leader. Yvonne White and Lorne White performed at the 1988 Olympics in Calgary.

WILLIAM HALL

illiam Hall was born in Horton Bluff, Nova Scotia, in 1827. William was the son of Black Refugees who fled to Nova Scotia after the War of 1812. From an early age, he knew he wanted to work on the water, and worked in the shipyards in Hantsport, Nova Scotia, for several years, building wooden ships for the merchant marines. As a teenager, William joined the crew of a trading vessel and visited most of the world's most important ports before his eighteenth birthday.

Craving more adventure, William enlisted in the British Royal Navy in 1852, the same Navy that gave his parents their freedom during the War of 1812. Five years later, in 1857, he was aboard the HMS *Shannon* on his way to China. Halfway through the journey, the ship was ordered to switch courses to provide backup at the Fort of Lucknow in India—a mutiny was underway. The rebels had taken over the fort and were laying siege to the surrounding area.

When the *Shannon* arrived, they were met with intense gunfire. William and his lieutenant continued to load and fire a 24-pound gun at the walls of the fort, even after the rest of their party had been killed or injured. They inched closer and closer, pushing the enemy out. Just when it seemed like they would not make it, reinforcements appeared, allowing them to complete their mission and reclaim the Fort of Lucknow.

For his bravery, William became the first Black person, the first Nova Scotian, and the third Canadian to receive the **Victoria Cross**. In 1876, William retired and returned to Nova Scotia to live a quiet life on a farm in Avonport with his sisters. In 1901, when he appeared in a parade of British veterans, donning his Victoria Cross and three other service medals, the Duke of Cornwall and York (who later became King George V) noticed the medals and wanted to find out more about William. While it may have taken several years, William was finally being recognized for his bravery. In 2010, he was honoured with a Canadian postage stamp.

MARELENE CLYKE

In 1951, seventeen-year-old Marelene Clyke was looking for summer work in her hometown of Halifax and stores refused to hire her. She found out about the Canadian Women's Army Corps and realized that may be one of the only ways she was going to make any money. Marelene enlisted as a **reservist** *and became one of the first Black women from Nova Scotia to join the army reserves. Other girls from her neighbourhood joined along with her, in the hopes of earning money for school supplies and new clothes. Marelene got married in 1957 and retired from service as a corporal in 1958. She worked for the government after her retirement and her husband served in the military for thirty-one years. Marelene paved the way for other women to be able to freely and proudly serve their country.*

JEREMIAH JONES

eremiah Jones was a soldier, farmer, and truck driver from Truro, Nova Scotia. Jeremiah was a private with the 106th Battalion (Nova Scotia Rifles) Canadian Expeditionary Force during the First World War. During the **Battle of Vimy Ridge** in France, Canadian troops were pinned down by German machine-gun fire. Jeremiah volunteered to attack a German gun nest and tossed a grenade, which killed seven German soldiers. The remaining soldiers surrendered. He commanded the surrendered soldiers to carry their machine guns across Canadian lines and drop them at the feet of his commanding officer.

For his bravery, Jeremiah was recommended for a Distinguished Conduct Medal by his commanding officer, an award he never received in his lifetime. On February 22, 2010, sixty years after his death, Jeremiah was posthumously awarded a Canadian Forces Medallion for Distinguished Service.

DID YOU KNOW?

Jeremiah enlisted with the 106th Battalion in 1916 when he was fifty-eight years old, thirteen years above the age limit. When he registered as a volunteer, he wrote his birthday was March 29, 1877, which would have made him thirty-nine years old.

MAJOR WALTER PETERS

**W**hen Walter Peters took to the skies in 1963, he became Canada's first Black jet fighter pilot and air force flying instructor. Growing up, Walter was the youngest of six children. His family moved from Litchfield, Nova Scotia, to Saint John, New Brunswick, when he was a young boy.

Walter rose above poverty and racism and was awarded a scholarship to Mount Allison University in New Brunswick. While there, he focused on earning an engineering degree and playing on the university's football team, but others on campus were focused on his race. Some of his classmates refused to room with him in residence because he was Black, but that didn't stop Walter from making a name for himself on the football field. He was the fastest running back of his day and was named both Rookie of the Year and the league MVP. Walter also met his wife, Nancy, a white woman from Sackville, New Brunswick, while attending university. It was extremely difficult to be an interracial couple in the 1960s. Many people didn't think a Black man should be with a white woman, but Walter and Nancy were in love and were determined to be together whether everyone agreed with it or not.

In the early 1960s, when he was twenty-four years old, Walter enlisted in the Royal Canadian Air Force and began training to become a pilot. As the first Black man in the field, Walter was a trailblazer. Not everyone welcomed him with open arms, but Walter stuck to his mantra: *You don't have to accept me, but you do have to respect me.*

More respect came after Walter's first solo flight in a Chipmunk aircraft, which was a two-seater, single-engine plane. After arriving safely back on the ground after that first flight, he was met by his fellow air force pilots, who were eagerly waiting with a pair of scissors. This was an air force tradition: after soloing an aircraft for the first time, pilots had their ties cut off and pinned to a board in the mess hall. He was now part of the team.

Walter went on to become the Canadian Armed Forces' first human-rights officer. Anyone who felt their rights were violated as a member of the armed forces would come to Walter and he would investigate their complaint. Walter was also an adviser to the United Nations Security Council. The council is focused on maintaining peace around the world and making sure people feel safe. Walter also helped in the development of the Canadian Snowbirds, the military's high-flying aerobatic team. Walter spent two years flying as a Snowbird himself, and called it a highlight of his long aviation career.

PART VI

A FEW FIRSTS

66 *If I could teach one thing to the next generation, it would be that no one should accept the status quo.* 99

–Daurene Lewis, former mayor of Annapolis Royal

66 *If you allow racism to break your spirit, you won't succeed—you can't let your spirit be broken. I'm here to serve. I am not going to allow racism to stop me from moving forward. Nothing stops me.* 99

–The Honourable Mayann Francis, former lieutenant-governor of Nova Scotia

A FEW FIRSTS

 pioneer is someone who does something that's never been done before, who paves the way for others and earns the title of "first." These individuals all achieved firsts in their fields—whether it's politics, science, sports, or the arts. They broke down barriers and did away with the status quo to create change and to make a difference.

It can be scary to do something that no one's done before you. What if you fail? What if nothing changes? But because these brave Black Atlantic Canadians were first, it meant that others who came after them could follow in their footsteps. And while being the very first at anything is amazing in itself, these individuals went even further and have left, or continue to leave, their mark on the world.

These men and women are the firsts, but because of their hard work, they certainly won't be the last.

PAUL GROWNS AND JEVAUGHN COLEY

n 2019 Paul Growns and Jevaughn Coley did something no other Black man or woman had done before them: they became the first Black police officers of the Royal Newfoundland Constabulary (RNC). Considering the RNC is almost three hundred years old and is North America's oldest civil police service, that's a pretty big deal!

Jevaughn was born in Kingston, Jamaica, and always dreamed of becoming a police officer. Jevaugn's mother came to Canada and became a daycare worker in city of St. John's. She wanted to give her children a better life and thought Canada was the best opportunity for them. It took some time to get adjusted to their new home and make new friends, but eventually Jevaughn began to settle into life in Canada and started setting goals for the future. His first job was at a local McDonald's restaurant, where he eventually became a manager. While he worked at McDonald's, Jevaughn also completed an Office Administration program at the College of the North Atlantic. For Jevaughn, each step brought him closer to fulfilling his dream of becoming a police officer.

Just like Jevaughn, Paul Growns, who lived in Canterbury, England, always wanted to be a police officer. But in the late 1980s, there was a height requirement for British police officers and Paul was too short to join. So he set his sights on the Royal Air Force and served for twenty-three years. For four of those years, he was stationed in Happy Valley-Goose Bay, Newfoundland and Labrador. Paul and his wife decided to call Canada their permanent home in 2013. At forty-eight years old, Paul achieved what he set out to do decades before. He was the oldest graduate in his class and was happy to be a mentor for some of the younger recruits, including Jevaughn.

While the paths they took to achieve their dreams may have been different, Paul and Jevaughn both share the same goal: to serve their community and keep the people of Newfoundland and Labrador safe.

MAYANN FRANCIS

Growing up in the diverse neighbourhood of Whitney Pier, Cape Breton, Mayann Francis and four of her six siblings were surrounded by immigrant families who hailed from all over the world. Mayann's father was a priest and her mother stayed home to look after the household and take care of Mayann and her brothers and sisters. The family didn't have much money, but they never felt poor. There was always food on the table and lots of love to go around. The church was an important part of Mayann's upbringing.

Mayann's mother and father always talked about the importance of education, which ignited Mayann's lifelong desire to learn. In 1999, Mayann was named the CEO of the Nova Scotia Human Rights Commission and was the first female ombudsman of Nova Scotia. Mayann always had big dreams and big ideas. She wanted to do exciting things in her life and get to a place where she could make a difference. Later that year, at a party with friends to celebrate the new millennium, all partygoers wrote on a piece of paper what they would like to achieve in the new century. Mayann had lots of ideas to jot down and she said she would achieve all of them when she became Lieutenant Governor of Nova Scotia. The Lieutenant Governor is appointed by the federal government to represent the Queen and perform different ceremonial duties in the province. To some it sounded far-fetched, but in 2006, Mayann became the first Black Nova Scotian and second Black Canadian Lieutenant-Governor of Nova Scotia.

As lieutenant-governor, Mayann accomplished another first. The Canadian government asked Mayann about granting a posthumous Free Pardon to Viola Desmond, sixty-four years later, erasing all charges that had been laid against Viola after her racist encounter at the Roseland Theatre in 1946. Mayann Francis was only three months old when the incident occurred.

DONALD OLIVER

onald Oliver and his four sisters and brothers never thought much about the fact that they were one of the few Black families living in Wolfville in the 1940s until someone every now and then would remind them that they didn't look like everyone else. Don's parents were quite strict, and all their children had chores around the home. One of Don's chores was helping his father in their garden. Don hated the pesky blackflies and was always eager to get the task done so he could play with his friends.

In the summer of 1962, when Don was in university, he travelled to Ethiopia with a group of Canadian and American youth to help rebuild a community that had been ruined by a drought. Don was eager to not only help, but also to learn about the country's people and hoped to find out more about his ancestors. That one life-changing experience ignited a flame inside the young university student and Don's been determined to give back and fight for human rights ever since.

Don's parents wanted him to study theology, but he chose law and eventually became a lawyer in Halifax. In 1990, former Prime Minister Brian Mulroney appointed Don to the Senate of Canada and he became the first Black Nova Scotian senator.

As a lawyer, businessman, and as a senator for twenty-two years, Don was proud to represent the people of Nova Scotia and work towards more diversity in the workplace and equality for all, no matter the colour of their skin. Don's work led him to meet another very important man who also shares those values. In 2009, while in the senate, Don had the honour of travelling to Washington and meeting President Barack Obama. The first Black Canadian man appointed to the Senate meeting the first Black US president was a pretty amazing moment that Don will never forget.

DID YOU KNOW?

Don's grandfather on his mother's side is William A. White, who was the chaplain of the No. 2 Black Construction Battalion. Don's half-brother, William P. Oliver, founded the Black Cultural Centre of Nova Scotia. His aunt is Portia White, the famed contralto. Don's mother was a well-known concert pianist who accompanied Portia.

WANDA THOMAS BERNARD

anda Thomas Bernard was born in East Preston, Nova Scotia. When she was just twelve years old, her father was killed in a car accident and her mother was left to care for her and her nine brothers and sisters. Days later, in Grade 8, Wanda started attending a non-segregated school. It was the first time she went to a school that had students of more than one race and she had to deal with racism on a regular basis. Wanda excelled in school, and when she was fifteen years old, she began taking courses at Mount Saint Vincent University. But her young age made it difficult to keep up with the older students and she ended up having to leave the university in her first year. She began working in the cafeteria at Dalhousie University to earn some money. Two years later, she returned to Mount Saint Vincent University and this time, she was ready. Wanda graduated with a bachelor's degree and then went on to earn her master's degree in social work from Dalhousie University and a Ph.D. from the University of Sheffield in England in 1996.

Wanda and her husband returned to East Preston to live because she missed her home. She missed neighbours dropping off food if someone was ill, and smiling faces on her walk to church. She missed the people coming together on stormy days to clear the roads. Unlike other communities in the Halifax Regional Municipality, East Preston didn't have the snow cleared from its streets, so members of the community would work together to make sure everyone had a clear path. East Preston was home and that is where Wanda wanted to live.

It was that sense of community and building one another up that inspired Wanda to become a social worker. She wanted to help people, just like people helped her after she lost her father when she was a child. People were there to support her family and gave her hope for a brighter future. It was time for her to pay it forward and be that bright light for others. Wanda worked to improve the welfare and services offered to Black families in Canada. In 1990, Wanda began to teach at the School of Social Work at Dalhousie University. She became the school's director in 2001 and held that role until 2011.

Wanda's work has been recognized on several occasions, including her receiving the Order of Canada in 2005 and the Order of Nova Scotia in 2014. In 2016, Wanda became the first Black Nova Scotian woman in the Senate of Canada.

DAURENE LEWIS

aurene Lewis was a seventh-generation descendant of Black Loyalists, and her ancestors include Rose Fortune (see page 18), who, like Daurene, worked hard to overcome racism to achieve success.

Daurene wanted to become a nurse who would travel all over the world. She wanted to explore Europe, the pyramids of Mexico, the Cedars of Lebanon, and the Great Wall of China. But instead, after becoming a registered nurse, Daurene ended up staying close to home and studied nursing education at Dalhousie University in Halifax. And it proved to be the best decision she ever made.

Daurene wanted to help and educate people. She also wanted to keep family traditions alive. While Daurene was living in Toronto, her mother became ill. After decades of weaving, Daurene's mother wasn't strong enough to continue her craft and decided to sell her looms. Daurene returned home to Annapolis Royal with the intent of learning everything she could about weaving and continuing her mother's passion in Toronto. But the people of Annapolis Royal had other plans. The local hospital offered Daurene a job as a nurse and different local businesses asked Daurene to assist them in their shops. Daurene could now be close to her mother, work on her looms, and earn a living in her hometown.

Daurene's weaving became rather popular and it wasn't long before she was selling the products that had started as a hobby and a way to keep her mother's passion alive. Daurene established herself as an important part of the community and her involvement eventually lead to her becoming a candidate for town council. She won a seat on the council in 1979 and was appointed deputy mayor in 1982.

In 1984, Daurene was elected mayor of Annapolis Royal, making her the first Black mayor in Nova Scotia and the first Black female mayor in Canada. In 1988, Daurene was the first Black woman in Nova Scotia to run in a provincial election. Although Daurene didn't win the election, she continued to serve her community. Like her ancestor Rose Fortune, Daurene made a name for herself and her legacy lives on. A sculpture of Daurene sits outside the Annapolis Royal town hall and is right across the street from the weaving shop she used to own. And each year the Daurene Lewis Memorial Award is given to a deserving student enrolled at the Nova Scotia Community College, who, just like Daurene, is making a difference in their community.

CORRINE SPARKS

Corrine Sparks's family lived in the tight-knit community of Lake Loon, Nova Scotia. Growing up with her eight brothers and sisters, the family didn't have much. Her parents put their children's needs ahead of their own and taught each of them the importance of education. In the 1970s, Corrine went to an integrated middle school. The Black students in the school weren't always treated fairly, but Corrine had a few Black and East Indian teachers who saw her potential and made sure she knew how much they believed in her. They took her to libraries and did trips to local universities.

In 1971, Corrine began an economics degree at Mount Saint Vincent University in Halifax. It was a big deal for a Black woman from a poor family to be attending university. It was made possible when her high school principal submitted her name to a local rotary club. The club offered to pay for some of Corrine's schooling. A few local nuns also wanted to help and they gave money to cover more of Corrine's tuition, as well as a place to live while she studied. Corrine wanted to be a history teacher. While she was studying, she took a summer job at the Nova Scotia Human Rights Commission. Her time with the commission sparked her interest in the law and she began thinking about how she could help fight the racism in her own community. After graduating from Mount Saint Vincent in 1974, she enrolled at Dalhousie Law School. There were one hundred and twenty students in her class and Corinne was one of only three other Black students. She was the only Black woman.

Corrine graduated in 1979. After graduation she ran the first all-female law firm in Nova Scotia with another lawyer named Helen Foote. The firm focused on family law.

On March 27, 1987, Corrine became the first Black judge appointed in Nova Scotia and the first Black female judge in all of Canada. Corrine says being the first is a big responsibly and she handles each case with fairness and justice in mind.

In November 2020, Corrine received the Weldon Award for Unselfish Public Service from Dalhousie University's Schulich School of Law.

WAYNE ADAMS

**W**ayne Adams was only thirteen years old when his father passed away. His mother and other members of the community became his role models, mentors, and inspiration. Community leaders like Reverend William Pearly Oliver encouraged him to work hard, dream big, and perhaps most important of all, be kind to others.

Wayne was a man of many hats and tackled many different ventures throughout his life. His first full-time job was at a Halifax Chevrolet dealership. Wayne eventually became the manager of Nova Scotia's first indoor car service station and was the first Black owner/operator of a Shell service station. He was also a broadcaster and provided national coverage of Canada's very first summer games in 1969. The opening ceremonies were held at Saint Mary's University's Huskies Stadium. From 1972 to 1978, he hosted a radio show called *Black Journal*, about current affairs and issues that affected Black Canadians. Wayne also had a Sunday morning gospel show on a community radio station.

When Wayne announced he would run for the provincial election in 1993 in his riding of Preston, some people told him politics was no place for a Black man and tried to convince him not to run. The naysayers just made Wayne want to run for and win a seat in Province House.

And he did just that.

Wayne became the first Black person in Nova Scotia to be elected to the **Legislative Assembly** and the first and only Black cabinet minister for the Province of Nova Scotia. The cabinet is selected by the premier, and each minister is assigned a department within the government, like health, employment, or immigration.

Cabinet ministers make decisions within their department on issues and policies that will affect the public. When Wayne was named to Liberal premier John Savage's cabinet as minister of the environment, the people who supported him far outnumbered those who first tried to dissuade him from running. When others heard the good news, he received more than three hundred telephone messages on his home answering machine, and over four hundred letters and cards from well wishers from all over the world.

In his role as minster of environment, Wayne focused on making a cleaner and safer environment for Nova Scotia families and protecting the province's beautiful forestland. He stopped municipal dumps from being built near low-income families and introduced the Protected Spaces Act, which made sure nearly eight thousand acres of land would never be destroyed. In 1995, Wayne encouraged Nova Scotians to reduce, reuse, and recycle. He created a solid-waste management strategy that lowered the amount of landfill waste by 50 percent. Less garbage going into landfills meant less pollution going into the surrounding rivers and streams. Wayne's environment initiatives were used around the globe to make the earth cleaner and greener.

While Wayne did a lot as a politician, he was also an active member of his community and was a part of several organizations. He was a founding member of the Black Cultural Society of Nova Scotia and was executive director of the Black Cultural Centre. Wayne visited schools across the province to talk about racism and the importance of treating others with respect and dignity. For all of these reasons and more, in 2004 Wayne was awarded the Order of Canada. Whether it was through his environmental work or his activism in his community, Wayne always has one goal in mind: to make the world a better and more beautiful place for future generations.

LINDELL SMITH

Lindell Smith has fond memories of watching his grandmother pick blueberries and the sweet smell of fresh bread baking in her kitchen. When Lindell was a teenager, he attended a public high school in the city of Halifax that brought in students from all races and classes. Lindell made sure he spoke with people who came from different backgrounds instead of only hanging out with the kids who were just like him. He wanted to step outside of his comfort zone and learn about other people.

Lindell never really thought about running as a Halifax city councillor, but when a seat became available, most of the people

Amazing Black Atlantic Canadians

he spoke with thought he would be the perfect candidate. He loved North End Halifax, he'd done public speaking since he was twelve years old, he had plenty of ideas on how things could be done differently, and he wanted kids to know that anyone can do great things in their community.

When Lindell finally decided to run as a city councillor he was sure of one thing: he wanted to be himself. He didn't want to change the way he dressed, he didn't want to cut his hair, and he didn't want to become someone else just so people would like him. He knocked on a lot of doors and met a lot of different people. Some were very supportive and happy to vote for Lindell, while others told him they wouldn't vote for someone who looks like him.

In 2016, Lindell Smith was elected to the Halifax city council and became the first Black city councillor in sixteen years. And at twenty-six years old, he was also one of the youngest. Lindell's passion for helping the younger generation is apparent through the non-profit recording studio he co-founded called Centreline Studio. The space welcomes youth who want to express themselves through art and music. Lindell wanted to change the way people view politicians and he's done that just by being himself.

IMPORTANT DATES

BEFORE 1605: Mathieu da Costa is recorded as the first free Black person to set foot on Canadian soil.

1775–1783: Enslaved Black people from American southern states are promised freedom if they fight for Britain during the American Revolution.

AFTER 1783: 3,500 Black Loyalists and 1,500 enslaved Black servants arrive in Nova Scotia and New Brunswick.

1784: The Black Pioneers, an all-Black regiment, build Birchtown, Nova Scotia.

1787: A colony where formerly enslaved Black people can live in freedom is established in Sierra Leone, Africa.

1792: 1,200 Black Loyalists sail from Halifax to Sierra Leone.

1796: The British government transports 600 Jamaican Maroons to Halifax.

1800: Approximately 550 Jamaican Maroons leave Halifax and sail for Sierra Leone.

1812: America declares war on Britain and attacks Canada. Many American refugees join the fight on the British/Canadian side.

1814: After the War of 1812, 2,000 Black American war veterans settle in Nova Scotia and New Brunswick.

1834: Britain abolishes slavery in Canada and all other colonies.

1867: Canada east (Quebec), Canada west (Ontario), New Brunswick, and Nova Scotia join to create the Dominion of Canada. This is known as Confederation.

1917: The all-Black No. 2 Construction Battalion sails for service in France.

1960s: The Black community of Africville, near Halifax, is destroyed.

1995: February is declared Black History Month (now known as African Heritage Month) across Canada.

GLOSSARY OF TERMS

American Revolutionary War (1775–1783): a war in the 18th century between Great Britain and its thirteen colonies. The colonies declared their independence as the United States of America and allied with France.

Battle of Vimy Ridge (April 9–12, 1917): fought during the First World War in northern France and noted as Canada's most celebrated military victory. For three days, the Canadian Corps attacked the ridge and captured it from the German army. More than 10,600 Canadians were wounded and/or killed during the attack.

Canadian Charter of Rights and Freedoms: a legal document that guarantees certain rights and freedoms to Canadian citizens.

civil lawsuit: when someone holds someone else responsible for a wrongdoing and expects justice or compensation in court.

colour barrier: for many years, minority groups were separated and not given the same rights and opportunities as other races. This was reflected in sports, restaurants, schools, jobs, and even the simple act of getting a haircut.

company: this is a military term that typically consists of 80 to 150 soldiers and is usually commanded by a major or captain.

discrimination: unjust treatment based on a number of identifiers, such as skin colour, age, ability, or gender.

Amazing Black Atlantic Canadians

emancipation: the process of being freed from slavery.

freedom songs: also called "civil rights anthems," these are powerful songs about being freed from slavery that were sung or chanted by marchers, activists, and participants during the civil rights movement of the 1950s and 60s.

Government House: the official residence of the lieutenant-governor of Nova Scotia.

Governor General Award: a prestigious award presented by the governor general of Canada to deserving individuals who have excelled in numerous academic, artistic, and social fields.

Harry Jerome Awards: an award honouring excellence in African Canadian sporting achievement named for the track and field athlete and teacher from Prince Albert, Saskatchewan. Harry Jerome was a three-time Olympian who won a bronze medal in the 100-metre race at the 1964 Summer Games in Tokyo, Japan. He won gold medals at the 1966 Commonwealth Games and the 1967 Pan American Games. When he was just eighteen years old, Harry broke the Canadian record in the 220-yard dash.

indentured servants: men and women who signed a contract to agree to work for a certain number of years in exchange for food, clothing, shelter, and sometimes freedom.

Legislative Assembly: a member of the legislative assembly (MLA) is a representative elected by the public in a designated area to the legislature. Among other roles, the legislature makes laws and controls provincial public spending.

ombudsman: a legal representative who is appointed by the government to investigate complaints made by individuals.

poet laureate: a person appointed by the government to compose poems for special occasions.

posthumous pardon: when someone is symbolically and officially redeemed (usually of a crime) after they have died.

racial segregation: setting someone apart from other people because of the colour of their skin.

racism: when a group of people are treated unfairly due to the colour of their skin. Sometimes this unfair treatment even results in harmful words or violence.

reservist: a member of the military reserve forces. The reserve force is a military organization whose members are citizens of a country and who work in the military as well as outside of the military.

systemic racism: systems or structures (within companies, schools, or governments) that have rules in place that exclude or disadvantage a particular group based on race.

valedictorian: a student who typically excels in academics and is voted by his or her teachers and/or peers to give a speech at the graduation ceremony.

Victoria Cross: the highest and most prestigious award of the British honours system. Awarded for great bravery and sacrifice.

FURTHER RESOURCES

BOOKS

Africville by Shauntay Grant and Eva Campbell

Birchtown and the Black Loyalists by Wanda L. Taylor

Marjorie Turner-Bailey Can Run (Her Journal) by Marjorie Turner-Bailey

Mayann Francis: An Honourable Life by Mayann Francis

That Lonesome Road: The Autobiography of Carrie M. Best by Carrie Best

The Black Battalion 1916-1920: Canada's Best-Kept Military Secret by Calvin W. Ruck

They Called Me Chocolate Rocket: The Life and Times of John Paris, Jr., Hockey's First Black Professional Coach by John Paris, Jr.

Soul Man: The Rocky Johnson Story by Rocky Johnson and Scott Teal

Winds of Change: The Life & Legacy of Calvin Ruck by Lindsay Ruck

WEBSITES

blackhistorycanada.ca

thecanadianencyclopedia.ca

FILMS

Honour Before Glory by Anthony Sherwood

Portia White: Think on Me by Sylvia Hamilton

ACKNOWLEDGEMENTS

**W**riting this book was a team effort and I'm thankful to everyone who helped me along the way.

I'm so grateful to Nimbus Publishing for being as excited as I am about this book. It has always been a dream of mine to write for younger readers, so thank you to Whitney Moran and Terrilee Bulger for believing in my abilities to work on such an important project. Editing a book is just as important as writing a book, so I'd like to thank my editor, Emily MacKinnon, for her patience and her great attention to detail.

A big thank you to everyone who answered my e-mails and phone calls when I needed to double-check important dates, names, and numbers. Thank you for taking the time to make sure I got the information right so I could tell people's stories to the best of my ability.

Thank you so much to artist James Bentley, who put so much love into each and every one of the illustrations in this book. You brought these pages to life and I'm thankful for this partnership with you.

I do everything with my family in mind and they are my biggest inspiration. Thank you for always encouraging me to do what I love.

And finally, to the people who fill these pages. They are trailblazers, they are change-makers, and they are truly amazing. They paved the way so future generations can dream big, reach for the stars, and be proud Black Atlantic Canadians. For that, I am truly grateful. Thank you.

INDEX